Endineering.

Ends: Why we overlook endings for humans, products, services and digital. And why we shouldn't.
Published 2017
Available on Amazon.

Cover illustration by Joe Macleod.

ISBN. 978-91-639-4783-4

For more information on Endineering go to
www.andend.co

Endineering.

Designing consumption lifecycles that end as well as they begin.

Joe Macleod
2021

Contents.

Preface.

The Ends book came out in 2017. Ever since it's been non-stop endings for me - conferences, training, writing, podcasts, articles and working with businesses. This has been successful in raising awareness of a lack of responsible, reflective conclusions in our consumer experiences. I had revealed something important. As one conference review said

> "Joe re-wired my brain. It's not often that such a big idea and way of thinking is hiding in plain sight."

Indeed, it was an important story about consumerism that doesn't often get told. The Ends book shone a light on a biased consumer experience that championed increased consumption over good endings. It was a story that went back centuries, with its early history in a 14th century, European, post-plague era. That saw relationships with religion, jobs and investments change.

This laid the foundations for a consumer mindset that the industrial revolution was poised to exploit. Individuals worked more, to buy more and reflect on the consequences less. New techniques in marketing helped create sophisticated, informed and driven consumers. They could navigate enormous complexity when making purchase decisions, yet failed to know where their trash was sent or how to delete a Tweet. The Ends book examined this issue through history and across industrial sectors, showing how even new landscapes of consumerism have also adopted this ending-less approach.

The Ends book told the reader why we don't do endings in consumerism. But knowing why isn't enough to solve the problem. The Ends book was only the beginning. Additional work was needed. Over the following years I developed the themes, providing increased structure, matured methods and identified characteristics. These were developed into training programmes that I ran all over the world with people from product development, design, sustainability, and businesses. These got better and better and in the last year I have been assembling them into a new how-to book. **The Endineering book tells the reader how-to create good endings.**

Acknowledgements.

Over the last few years of evangelising endings, I have come to appreciate the help of a disparate group of people working across disciplines and scattered all around the world. Their only linkage is a common feeling that the current approach to the consumer experience is missing something. And maybe it is the end.

There are individuals who I want to call out in particular for their support: My wife Alex, who is an inspiration, and such an enormous foundation to all of my life. My editor, Monica, who has been supportive, insightful, and knowledgeable, not to mention very tolerant of my terrible dyslexic-induced spelling and grammar. My brother, Alistair, who has been an inspiring champion of causes around sustainability and a constant sage for advice on the consequences of consumerism.

I would like to thank the reviewers of the book, who laboured through drafts and provided such valuable and insightful feedback – Gillian Crampton Smith, Task Willcocks, Martin Dowson and James Wallman.

I want to also thank the people who gave up their time to be interviewed and share their story about endings –Mathias Wikstrom and Johan Pihl from Doconomy. Amanda Molina Zoppas, who talked about the circular vacuum cleaner from Electrolux. Harry Brignull who talked about his work with Dark

Patterns. Louise Klemens, and Soren Hartvig Laursen, who talked about the Beautiful Exit from 3 Denmark. And Alex Crowfoot who talked about his project on a retirement village through the context of endings.

A further group of people I want to thank are all the amazing people who have supported the theme of ends and see it as a valuable approach to changing the consumer life-cycle for the better.

The interaction design world that has been very supportive in getting the message out. Particularly the IXDA community and all its local groups who have invited me to talk. Also, Euro IA, UX Salon, MOBx, World Usability Day, UX Cambridge, UX London, UX Scotland, UX Australia, UXLx Portugal, UX Live London and many more. Thanks.

From the tech and digital product world: Product Camp Poland, Digital K Bulgaria, Camp Digital Manchester, Canvas Conference Birmingham, WebExpo Prague. Thank you.

From the service design world: Service Design Network, Netherlands and Spain, Service Design for Business London, Service Design Collective New York. Thank you.

From education and design organisations: Jenny Theolin and Tash Willcocks, at Berghs and Hyper Island, Clive Grinyer at the Royal College of Art, Ashley at Falmouth University, Graham at California College of Arts, Karin at The Talent Institute, Umea Design School, Nackademin, Hochshule Luzern Switzerland, Design Council London, AIGA New York. A big thanks to all of you.

From the customer experience and marketing world: James Wallman and the WXO, Off Grid Sessions UK, MediaCom London, Future of Customer Experience Conference London, Customer Loyalty Conference Sweden.

From the training and personal development world: Lauren Currie and Upfront, Andrew Mina and Eloomi.

From the financial services world: Credit Strategy London, MarksWebb Moscow, Swedbank Stockholm, Lending Summit London, Lloyds Bank London, Credit Summit London

From the world of sustainability: Disruptive Innovation Festival by Ellen MacArthur Foundation UK, Sustainable UX US, Circularity 21 US.

And the many, many, businesses who have invited me to talk: Ustwo, Google Deep Mind, Wolff Olins, Facebook, Fjord, Co Op, Lloyds Bank, Method, Futureheads, JP Morgan, Auto Trader, Tata Consultancy, Huawei, PepsiCo, Intuit, iZettel, PayPal, Net-a-Porter, Doberman, BT, Arup, Spotify, Ikea, The Collective, Arrival, Just Eat and Sky, to name a few.

The issue of ends.

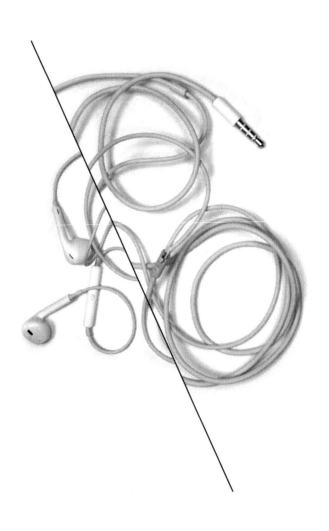

Ch.1
Introduction.

Many of us feel lost. Trapped in the oscillation between consumerism and concern. At one end are powerful short-term individualistic desires satisfied by consumerism. At the other the guilty experience of an overburdened environment and society. To improve this, we are told to consume more - buy more of the *"right"* things, engage more, post more images. Yet, still the world heats up, pollution increases, and social media gets more toxic. But maybe the answer isn't in doing more? Maybe it is at the end?

At the start of the consumer lifecycle, we celebrate new products, showering them with our attention. Whole industries are focused on the beginning of the consumer lifecycle. The consumer's behaviour is monitored through infinite lenses – the aim is to nudge their emotions, gain attention and finally make a sale. The products purchased have been crafted to be the best they can be. The purchases are meant to fulfill infinite consumer desires across broad wants and needs. This is where human endeavour is concentrated—making, selling and consuming.

The end of the consumer lifecycle is a different matter. The consumer is left abandoned, alone and un-instructed. The language they hear is cold and functional, delivered by societal representatives such as municipal waste companies, legislation and campaign groups. This inspires emotions such as shame about plastic in the sea, fear about our reduced privacy in digital or confusion about the long-term exposure of a financial services product.

The end needs to be an active part of the consumer experience. The ideal would be to glue the aspirational desires of consumption together with responsibility and reflection of a good ending. This should be an ambition for all of us – as consumers, as producers, as businesses, as policy leaders.

As consumers, we need to look beyond the excitement of purchase and usage to ask the question *"How does it end?"*. Personally, since looking at endings, I now consider everything I buy through the lens of ends. I hope that reading this book will inspire you to ask that question too.

In addition, this book proposes some foundational questions that need to be addressed globally by policy and governments. It also gives details of approaches that could be adopted by many businesses around culture and strategy. Much of the book provides practical tools and guidance for those working on product development and the consumer experience.

To speak to these audiences, I have broken the text into four sections.

- The first section frames the problem in simple terms by establishing some key issues.
- The second section aims to frame the issues around the individual consumer.
- The third section looks at the issues from a business point of view.
- The fourth, and largest section, provides a guide to how to create better endings for the consumer experience with models, techniques, and processes.

On-boarding   Usage

The start and duration of the relationship

Language of self actualisation

Fuelled by commerce

Actionable and engaging

Attention and loyalty

Individualistic desires

Off-boarding

The end of the relationship

Language of safety and security

Fuelled by society

Guilt and repulsion

Abandoned, un-instructed

Societal and environmental responsibility

broke between beginning... and the end.

Ends and the consumer.

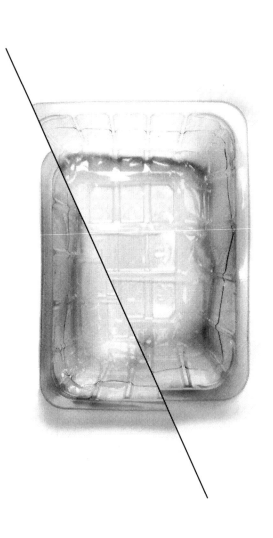

Ch. 2

The end gap.

The issue of consumerism is complicated. To clarify endings within this fog, I want to identify a gap which is made up of fundamental problems. This gap happens between the consumer's regular usage of the product and its end or demise. At this stage the engagement of the consumer with their product fades, activities lessen, interest wanes.

This gap has four commonly-observed characteristics. Jointly, they generate a vacuum of meaning and purpose in the consumer experience, which limits any improvement or positive action at the end of the consumer lifecycle. This has the potential for laying the foundation for many, wider, critical ills in consumerism.

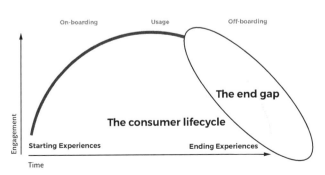

1/4

The consumer - provider relationship breaks

What began as a comfortable bonding between consumer and provider tumbles out of control as engagement fades. Either party might seek the end of the relationship, for any manner of reasons. The break in this partnership also breaks joint responsibility for the assets of the relationship. Society, through its wider functions such as legislation, waste management or consumer protection, is then left to pick up the broken pieces.

When the relationship is intact, the provider and consumer work on issues together. For example, in the Initial stages the provider normally gives instructions and guides usage. At off-boarding this signal weakens, thus leaving the consumer alone, uninstructed and unsupported.

The provider, meanwhile, loses a source of information and feedback. When the relationship is current, communication creates a data flow that informs product improvements. But this link fades as the end approaches.

The provider has deep knowledge about the assembly and materials in their products. When the relationship breaks, the provider loses access to the consumer and with it the ability to instruct the consumer, reclaim the assets and materials involved in the consumer engagement.

2/4

Asset definition is lost

At the end of the consumer lifecycle people seek out convenient solutions for disposal. For example, throwing physical products in the trash or deleting an app without closing the account. When this happens, the definition of the material waste is lost. It merges with other waste products, from other failed and ended consumer engagements, thus creating a mass of unknown elements. These assets become generic, lose identity, and are merged with other assets. This also reduces the ability to measure the impact of consumption.

The physical elements of a product relationship often require accurate disposal. Data might need clearing up or payments completed to close accounts properly.

Between the beginning and the end of the consumer relationship, definitions are focused on benefitting the short term aims of the original sale. The material knowledge and language required at off-boarding is rarely talked about in the relationship beforehand. How to dispose of a new phone won't be mentioned at on-boarding. What types of plastics a pen is made from won't be detailed at purchase.

The consumer often has to act independently at this point. They need to dispose of their own assets, uninstructed by the provider. Guidance about how to do it now falls to society. This guidance will be expressed in generalist terms, due to the overwhelming quantities that need to be disposed of.

3/4
Actors and actions are anonymised

Alongside the loss of the relationship between the consumer and the provider, there is the loss of identity attached to the assets used in the consumer experience. At the end of a physical product's life, consumer ownership is relinquished, thus detaching the identity of the consumer from the long-term impact of their consumption.

In data relationships, consumer assumptions about identity removal at the end are misplaced when data is sold on or amalgamated with other data sources. Data is often being re-attached in the background, quite unknown to the consumer. Thereafter they might experience covert engagements with third parties, like targeted advertising.

4/4

Routes to neutralising are blurred

Consumer society has been indulged with the idea, arguably over centuries, that consumption can have few negative consequences. Increasingly over the last few decades society has recognised this delusion. Consumers throw items away far too easily. This makes for bad choices at the off-boarding experience.

Consumer waste is taken from the home, out of state, beyond borders and shipped away to countries with lower recycling standards. A similar approach is taken for carbon neutralising. Companies and countries who fail to curtail their own carbon can easily offset it by investing in remote schemes in far-away countries.

As a consumer experience, the clarity of neutralising is blurred and distant. Examples such as recycling, data deletion or credit ratings can have false conclusions. Long term impact remains undefined, lacking permanence and failing to be neutralized.

Issues also surface in homes as consumers hoard old unused items that lack clear, safe routes to disposal. This results in the increase of off-site storage, hoarding of e-waste and digital assets.

These four characteristics of off-boarding in the consumer lifecycle entrench critical problems with consumerism. Their consequences cause widespread damage to the environment, personal privacy, and social cohesion. On one side of this gap is a buoyant individual experience of consumption. On the other side of the gap is the worst aspect of consumerism.

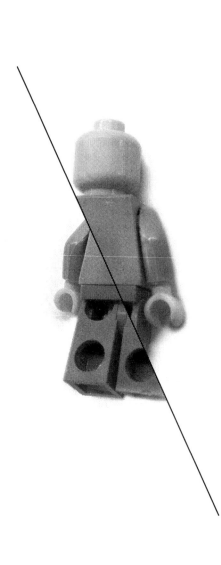

The Ch.3 consumer split.

When it comes to consumption, we have two conflicting personalities that work against one another - our consuming self, and our civil self. Their experiences are supported by separate embedded systems. The battleground is the customer experience and improving the negative impact of consumption. The two personalities are in silent, unconscious conflict.

One of these personalities is an active member of society, doing things on behalf of the community, concerned about the general wellbeing of others. Through this lens we worry about the environment, feel slighted by big corporations who process our data for ads, help our neighbours, save for the next generation, and conscientiously separate our re-cycling.

In contrast, the other personality, the consuming self, indulges dreams about purchasing new products and services, blinkered to the personal impact on the environment. That consuming self loves the thrill of getting the right product that fulfils the dream. And when that product is exhausted, broken, or comes to an end, it doesn't dwell on it. It removes it as quickly and conveniently as possible and then looks for a new one.

Systematic blinkering

These two selves avoid one another. This is easy as the systems that they live in every day rarely reference one other.

The consuming self lives in the commercial system of the customer life cycle, which encourages self-satisfaction, and consumption. It absorbs the tools of advertising and marketing, designed to flatter the user into making the next selfish purchase.

The civil self lives in the altruistic system of the community, which encourages responsible thinking, neighbourliness, and concerns itself with the environment and globalisation. The civil self uses the tools of democracy and citizenship to lobby governments, create community programmes and raise awareness about being better citizens.

The Consumer Self

The Civil Self

Protecting bad behaviour

When consuming, the consuming self is protected from the civil self. The commercial system avoids talking about issues that will alert the civil self to its consuming actions, for fear it will put the consuming self off their consumption. To do this, the customer lifecycle is punctuated by messages that reinforce the selfish good feelings of consuming. This could be reassurance that the product is right for them, how to use the product correctly, what makes it high quality or the best deal. Every aspect of the customer life-cycle reinforces the consuming self, apart from what happens when usage ends.

Once broken, outdated, or unfashionable, the product is no longer an issue for the consuming self. The handover takes place, and it becomes the problem of the civil self. This self needs to deal with things like broken electronics, shutting old email accounts, redundant cleaning products and the exhausted batteries of broken toys, among the other weekly rituals of waste or recycling.

The cliff of consumption

Currently, the consuming self pushes the problem off a cliff of consumption down on to our passive civil self to deal with. The consuming self, and the mechanism that supports it, have little interest in putting these two experiences together.

Conversely, the civil self finds it hard to talk the same language that the consumer self uses. The translation often ends up sounding like guilt.

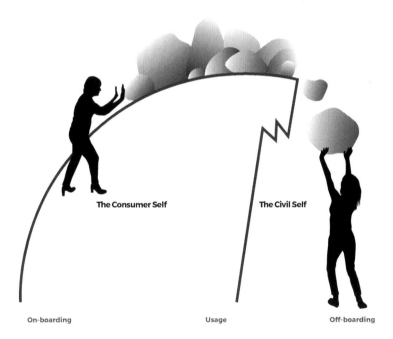

The Consumer Self   The Civil Self

On-boarding   Usage   Off-boarding

Resolving your personal differences

One of the victims of this situation is the individual, split into two personalities. Both of them lack a common language and framework to resolve the biggest problems with consumerism. Building a bridge between these two through common experience is critical. They need to build an area with joint purpose, language, and responsibilities. The end of the consumer lifecycle offers this opportunity.

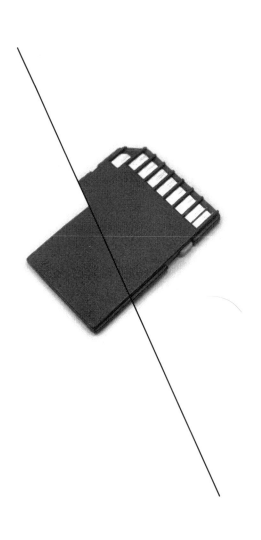

Measuring the end.

At the end of the consumer lifecycle, people need a common means of measurement to communicate the outcome of the engagement. This can help assess impact, set responsible limits and envisage the neutralising of any fall out.

Elsewhere in the consumer relationship, measurement is common. Such systems inform the consumer and provider about value in the relationship. They are used in different ways to provide leverage and encouragement.

Some systems are better at communicating on-boarding and usage periods than helping to inform knowledge at the off-boarding. We will look through a variety of these and their strengths in helping to measure consumption at the end.

Consumer values

There is a wealth of values that can be employed to measure consumers. Most are looking for a change in the consumer's behaviour. An article in Customer Strategist details the types of measurements and quantity of businesses using them. '32 *percent use lifestyle changes, such as a change in employment, a new household address, or the birth of a child; 58 percent use lifetime value drivers, such as changes in the frequency of purchases or changes in the mix of products bought; 42 percent use behavioural cues, such as receiving a complaint or signing up for a newsletter; and 64 percent use attitudes, such as satisfaction or willingness to recommend the company."[1]*

These types of measurement are well established. They have been developed through loyalty schemes and by monitoring purchasing habits using banking cards. They are linked to the individual consumer and captured on databases. In the event of a change, a trigger will action a new response from the business. This might be an email with an offer that acknowledges the situational change. This could be described as a dynamic system of cause and effect.

Most of the techniques are based on consumer purchases and are often blinkered to the consumer endings of those purchases.

Credit rating

To be an active consumer often requires a track record of managing money – or at least spending money. Having a bank account is but one aspect of that. A good credit score unlocks far more opportunities. Without it, a consumer is often stopped before they have started.

In financial agreements, reputation has driven trust for centuries, but a more universal, measurable credit score is a recent phenomenon. Not long ago, bank managers at local branches were in charge of distributing loans. This was risky and open to an individual's subjective judgement. Data from this model was erratic, to say the least, and predicting repayment was terrible.

It wasn't until the 1950's that Bill Fair, an engineer, and Earl Isaac, a mathematician, started to develop a measuring system to provide a single clear number for credit worthiness. It was based on a mix of five aspects of a person's credit activity: payment history, credit utilisation, length of credit history, new credit, credit mix.[2] Initially it failed to get adopted, but repeated efforts and crafting of the system by the pair saw it become the norm for the US credit industry. It is now known as the FICO Credit Rating, after the pair's company, Fair Isaac Corporation.

Credit scores were initially a secretive measurement, visible only to the banking and credit industry. In the last couple of decades, however, the information has been shared with consumers. An increased discussion about, and awareness of credit helps people adopt better credit behaviour. Increased digitisation, clearer language and better consumer tools now motivate people to keep their FICO rating in prime health.

Behavioural surplus

In the early 2000s Google was improving their approach to advertising. They had, of course, been monitoring their consumers and providing appropriate adverts, like any other business. That behavioural data was used to improve their products. They would measure as much as they could about users - location, sites visited, how long a person viewed images, etc. The list was enormous. But much was being measured in addition to the needs for product improvement. They started to see more opportunities, a surplus of knowledge that could do so much more than just improve ads.

In the following years, a newly-focused algorithm and a new vision for the company formed the basis for a new direction. Google went beyond observing behaviour to predicting behaviour. Shoshana Zuboff, author of Surveillance Capitalism and who some believe coined the term 'behavioural surplus', describes the impact of this new approach.

"Google uses your location data to target ads; indeed, these are among the most significant sources of surplus in Google's advertising markets with a direct impact on click rates. The standard account from Google and other surveillance capitalists is that behavioural surplus is retained only as metadata, which are then aggregated across large numbers of individual users. We are told that it's not possible to identify individuals from these large-scale amalgamations. However, with as little as three bits of data easily culled from the public record – birth date, zip code, and sex – reidentification science has demonstrated its ability to de-anonymise meta data with disturbing ease."[3]

Almost every aspect of a consumer's online activity is now measured by digital companies. It informs them of tiny details of an individual's life, thus enabling adverts to target with incredible nuances.

Of course, few consumers know that this constant measurement is being conducted. The experience on the surface of the interface gives little away of this larger intent. The consumer sees their unit of measurement in terms of 'likes' and 'follows', with little awareness of the thousands of other values being assigned to them as an individual.

An additional level of complexity is applied when this information is passed on to third parties. Whether through the use of cookies on websites, or direct behavioural observations via a platform like Facebook, a consumer's details can be distributed to thousands of destinations. Once there, it is unlikely the consumer knows or has influence to reclaim it or delete it.

Carbon off-setting

Human activity that creates emissions can be measured and expressed in tonnes of carbon dioxide equivalent. Companies or individuals can counterbalance their emissions by purchasing carbon off-sets of equal amounts. One tonne of carbon emissions is equal to one tonne of carbon off-set purchased. The off-set is linked to projects that are soaking up carbon - an example is planting trees.

Carbon off-sets don't just compensate for carbon dioxide. They also cover methane, nitrous oxide, per-fluorocarbons, hydrofluorocarbons, and sulphur hexafluoride. They also have common features that help provide legitimacy. The source of the off-set refers to the project that is making the off-set possible. This might, for example, be a re-forestation project in Ethiopia.

A certification regime describes what and who endorses the off-set. There are different companies which certify off-setting, thus providing some legitimacy to the scheme. Past schemes have lacked certification and thus undermined trust across the whole market. But recent improvements and a greater focus on this method of carbon reduction have helped build trust again.

There are two types of carbon off-sets. First, a compliance market, where companies can off-set the impact of their activities. Then there is a voluntary market, where individuals and smaller businesses can off-set their activities. For the compliance market, there are options for trading around the world. By far the most dominant is the European Union Emission Trading Scheme (EU ETS).[4]

The voluntary market for carbon off-setting is far more dynamic. Measurements for carbon usage by different companies can vary widely and prices to off-set fluctuate equally widely. This has plagued the market for off-setting alongside the take up by, and trust from consumers.

As a consumer experience, measuring carbon is difficult. It often requires a detailed knowledge of products, sourcing and fuels. In the past, details of consumption at this level have not been required for the consumer. They have often been limited to the provider for scientific or government use. With increased concern about the environment, there is more interest by consumers in measuring their carbon impact. New tools to capture activity have helped many people to do this. But it is still a long way from being common for people to know the extent of their personal carbon impact.

Measuring food consumption

Food ends up in two ways. It is either consumed, turning to energy or fat, or it is wasted. Measuring food consumption involves a variety of issues that are complex, technical and even political.

Calories are a common type of measurement used for food. They help people to recognise the impact of food choices on their weight. Developed by Nicolas Clément in 1819, calories became a common source of heat measurement. A calorie is the amount of energy needed to increase a volume of water by 1 degree. This is now commonly referred to as a KiloCalorie.

Tracking calories is quite a tricky undertaking for anyone. Even with clearer labelling on products, manual effort is needed to measure weights and quantities. To do this with accuracy and commitment is no small undertaking.

According to WebMD *"It is extremely difficult to count calories accurately. Although 67% of Americans report taking calories into account when making food purchases, nearly nine out of 10 have no idea how many they actually need."* [5]

WebMD cites a survey conducted by the International Food Information Council Foundation which said *"We tend to miscount what we eat. Although the U.S. food supply is 3,900 calories for each person per day, men claim to eat an average of 2,618 daily calories, while women report eating only 1,877."*

A glimmer of hope for measuring calories emerged in 2019 when a Russian start-up launched a product that promised to do it automatically. Healbe[6] claimed to be able track calories through the skin. The University of Davis Foods for Health Institute tested this with 27 volunteers. It reported that the device achieved 89% accuracy. Although this has yet to be peer reviewed and many people consider the quantity of subjects pretty low, it is a first step towards an automated calorie counter. This could lift the burden on the users who find it difficult to measure their food consumption. [7]

Measuring food waste

Food waste is a worldwide problem. According to ReFED, an American nonprofit charity. *"America wastes roughly 40 percent of its food."* 76 billion of that is household waste each year. *"In the US, an average person wastes 238 pounds of food per year (21 percent of the food they buy), costing them $1,800 per year."* [8]

China is similarly worried about the issue of food waste. According to the China Academy of Science up to *"18 million tonnes of food a year was wasted in large cities, enough to feed 30 to 50 million people a year."* [9]

A recent article in The Guardian followed the story of food waste in China, saying that the issue has become a higher priority in light of Coronavirus and a rise in the need to import rice to the country. The Chinese leader, Xi Jinping had issued a demand to change things and called for *"operation empty plate"*. He was targeting diners with the common belief that it is polite to order more than the amount needed when entertaining guests. The Guardian points out that *"Meals are often served family-style with shared dishes and hosts tend to order more dishes than the number of diners in the group. The Wuhan Catering Industry Association called on restaurants in the city to issue a system called "N-1 ordering" whereby a group must order one dish fewer than the number of diners."* [10]

A beef restaurant in the city of Changsha made their own interpretation of the campaign by setting up some scales in the front of their restaurant and asked people to weigh themselves before ordering. Accompanying the scales were posters saying *"Be thrifty and diligent, promote empty plates"* and *"Operation empty plate"*. The restaurant apologised after being shared 300 million times on the social platform Weibo. [11]

Putting aside the mass shaming of this exercise, measuring and enforcing changes through a common element - the plate - can be pretty impactful for restaurants in a police state. It provides clear evidence, universally understood at the end of the meal. But measuring everyday consumer experiences can be more complicated than that, especially at home, where the majority of wastage is happening.

Stopfoodwaste.ie, is a charity based in Ireland that promotes food waste prevention and home composting. Their practical recommendation for measuring food waste breaks down in to three sections. [12]

1. **Separate your food waste**

2. **Keep a record of what you throw out**

3. **Identify the reasons that you have thrown food out**

They point out that many of the items we dispose of with food waste will be the same each week, and often for the same reasons. Observing this is key to halting the behaviour and waste.

I would add here that consumerism is an emotional behaviour. So, it is worth digging deeper than just understanding the item that is being thrown out. Understanding the emotional attachment to the purchase at onboarding is important for breaking the cycle at source. Advertising and marketing, especially at point of sale, can manipulate the consumer's thinking. So, at off-boarding think of the emotions as well.

Measuring physical product ends

To measure the way in which we consume physical products would require a few different aspects to be measured. These could depend on whether the product is currently static in our home or has been disposed of. Therefore, it could be considered waste, recycling or clutter.

Hoarding

As I pointed out in the first Ends book, many consumers have terrible hoarding habits because of a lack of discussion, instruction and wider cultural norms about the end of the consumer lifecycle. This traps people with their products. According to Regina Lark, a professional organiser, the average US home contains around 300,000 things, from ironing boards to paperclips.[13] As we purchase more and more items, we fail to dispose of those we already have. We lack the resolve and the cultural mechanisms needed to off-board the old ones.

According to the neighbor.com, a storage search site, 9.4% of the US population uses self-storage. There is 1.709 billion sq. ft available across the US. Which, if dived, between the US population would provide 5.4 square feet per person. They put this in-to perspective by saying, *"there are more facilities than the combined count of Starbucks, McDonald's, Dunkin' Donuts, Pizza Hut and Wendy's restaurants!"*[14]

The TV show Storage Wars [15] show the auctioning of abandoned self-storage units. It's almost like a natural evolution of consumers not knowing what to do with things they don't need. Abandon them in a storage unit. Then abandon the storage unit.

Rubbish

This is officially called Municipal Solid Waste (MSW).[16] This is the sort of waste which is picked up by local councils or state-run municipal companies. Many countries that are working towards better forms of waste processing tend to have the highest outputs of waste. The World Bank estimates that the amount of rubbish created by humans globally increased from 0.64 kilograms on average per person in 2006 to 1.2 kilograms in 2016. This figure is estimated to rise to 1.42 kilograms by 2025. This is a frightening increase. But, if you dig deeper into the data, there might be hope as some countries advance their waste management processes – for example, the world's biggest producer of waste, Kuwait. Each of its 4 million inhabitants produce 5.72 kilograms per day, because of not having adequate waste processing.

Once better processing is in place, the World Bank predicts it will drop to 4 kilograms by 2025. [17]

The second biggest producer is Antigua, which generates 5.5 kilograms per capita. This is because of its reliance on tourism and lack of processing. Again, the World Bank predicts a drop to 4.3 kilograms by 2025.

St. Kitts comes in as the third biggest producer of waste in the world. This is currently at 5.45 kilograms per capita. The World Bank expects this to drop to 4 by 2025.

Waste plastic

It is estimated that around 20% of global plastic waste was recycled in 2015. But the trend is only estimated to get to around 44% by 2050. That leaves a lot of plastic unaccounted for. In 2010 it was estimated that the average American throws away about 12 ounces of plastic every day, which is the equivalent of about 26 average sized plastic bottles. [18]

As we can see, better processing can achieve better results in the end of a product's life. Many of these results seem to be investments into large scale processes and infrastructure. Yet it is clear that a great deal of the problem lies with the consumer. The breakdown in the consumer lifecycle happens at the end of the product's life. If the product can't get to the shiny new waste recycling plant, then the plant can't achieve its job. There are enormous opportunities for increasing waste management through better off-boarding and improved endings in the consumer lifecycle.

Engagement by people at this stage will achieve higher capture rates. The capture of plastic in many countries is starting to improve because of changes in the consumer experience. This has been demonstrated in PANT (a legal word referring to repayment later) schemes in Norway, which I will return to later in the book. Here nearly 90 percent of plastic used in bottles is recaptured through consumer engagement and the design of a proper off-boarding experience.

Social credit

Over the last few years, China has been testing a system of social credit. This is based on an individual's reputation across a number of factors and is intended to standardise the assessment of people and companies across the nation. Zhang Lifan, a prominent Chinese sociologist, suggests that the system will help increase trust across the country. *"There is a lack of trust across China, partly as a fallout of the Cultural Revolution, when people were pitted against* one another, even between neighbours, families and friends. It is believed that an impartial state-run system will help build trust back into society again." [19]

To operate this system China has invested significantly in the surveillance of its citizens with over 200 million surveillance cameras scattered over the country and nearly all its 1.4 billion citizens on its facial recognition data base. Few countries come as close to this level of citizen knowledge as China.[19] They are also leading innovation in this field, as they have filed nearly ten times more patents than the US in the face recognition sector.

The approach has received a lot of criticism from Western observers, who point out that individuals don't have a choice as to whether they are being assessed in the social credit scheme or not. It could, of course, be equally argued that big tech companies in the West are gathering similar quantities of information from consumers without the consumers having a clear understanding about being tracked.

One application of the Chinese social credit system is to measure how accurate people are when recycling. On July the 1st 2019, Shanghai started to implement garbage sorting regulations. Urban management officials would tour around the city's 4,000 waste disposal sites and measure the accuracy of rubbish sorting. According to the China Global Television Network *"Garbage classification is in fact now on China's national agenda, as the central government aims to have all cities, at and above prefecture level, establish a garbage sorting system by the end of 2025. Shanghai's rules, however, are referred to as the strictest regulation in history regarding garbage sorting. According to the new rules, individuals, who fail to properly separate their trash, face fines of up to 200 yuan, while businesses face fines up to 50,000 yuan (around 7,200 U.S. dollars)."*[20]

A future measurement of consumer impact

Measuring the end of the consumer lifecycle with a tangible, easy-to-understand unit would help the resolution of the engagement. It will help create justice in the consumer lifecycle. Making bad consumers and providers see their errors can endorse good consumers and providers.

There is a history of the measuring method valuing only active consumption. Credit rating, behavioural surplus, and a number of marketing measurements aim at valuing an active consumer. There has been less innovation in measuring the impact of the consumer and consequences of consumption. These measures have tended to be academic, scientific and beyond easy interpretation by the public.

More work needs to be done here to establish universal methods of measuring long term consumer impact. Carbon and calories are good examples, but they require significant effort by the consumer to engage. Other measures that are active in earlier phases of the consumer lifecycle are being assessed and improved all the time, capturing rich and detailed information about the consumer while active. The end of the consumer lifecycle is getting little attention as a place to measure.

Another issue is the longevity of these units of measure. Many are stopped once the consumer leaves the relationship, thus making it impossible to attach long term impact to the act of consumption or be able to see that impact dissipate over time. An important feature in any future unit of measurement would be that it is attached to the consumer beyond the consumer lifecycle. Despite China's social credit system being a questionable human rights violation, it does show capability for a long term, individual-based system that would recognise consumer impact beyond the engagement. This could be of significant benefit to the consumer themselves in terms of appreciating their long-term consumer behaviour.

Ch.5
Accountability and identity.

Year upon year we further subordinate our personal identities to commercial definition and ownership. While much of that commercial definition frames people as potential consumers or active customers, at the end of consumption individual identity is limited and blurred. It has got lost in the transition between active participant and passive witness of waste.

The first step might be to measure the impact of a consumer experience. Assigning that impact to an individual is the next. But there are significant challenges around this. Who owns the data on which the identity is built? How is data about consumption attached to an identity? How many of these systems are global?

On one hand, many people fear being monitored by a government authority, yet seem happy to give up large pieces of personal identity to commercial businesses. On the other hand, unless we start identifying personal roles in consumerism and build off-boarding experiences around that, we are unlikely to inspire behavioural change.

Historical Identity

Historically, knowledge of a person's identity would travel little further than the village they were born in. Identity was simple, tangible, local.

Family associations played a part - daughter of, son of. Further definitions were linked to the roles people played - the priest, the nurse, the baker. Authorities, principally the church, would capture peoples' identities formally by registering events such as births, deaths and marriages. In a similar way, governments would capture identities for the purpose of tax collection. More details could be added from the actions people performed and the views they held.

The means of capturing identity changed little over centuries until the Industrial Revolution. This increased industrial production consequentially increased the need for better sales. The whole concept of marketing matured and started to categorise different types of product and the people that consumed them. This early market segmentation empowered people in this new playground of identity, enabling them to manipulate themselves through their consumption.

Nitha Mathur, a professor of Sociology at the Indira Gandhi National University, explains it as *"Commercial brands and luxury commodities have come to serve as signifiers of identity in society and legitimised consumer culture that is made visible in terms of its referents: images, commodities and 'high-class' consumption as also their articulation in daily lives of people."* [1]

As new consumer sectors emerged, so data increased around peoples' identities. For instance, as banking services increased, information about their borrowing capability was attached to a person's identity. As medicine became better detailed and documented, so people became identified by their medical conditions. And most recently, the transition to digital has led to people being identified by their digital behaviour.

While such data provides a rich tapestry of detail about a person's behaviour and characteristics, more commonly the concentration is on their potential to consume. People are now defined by what they might buy and what they consume. What is not generally attached is the impact of their consumption.

Web cookies

'Accepting cookies' has now become a popular concept as people are confronted with the decision every time they encounter a new website. Cookies are used to capture small amounts of information from the computer of the user. Originally called *"magic cookie"* by developers working on Unix computers, it is a term for a packet of data a program receives and returns. [2]

Lou Montulli adapted the technology for use on web communication in 1994, including a shortened version of the word "*cookie*". The original intention was to help keep track of a partial browser state that developers didn't want to store on their own servers. They chose instead to store it on the user's machine. Cookies have been used commonly on the web ever since and are now a rich source of data capture for many advertising and tracking companies. Some of those companies are more sinister than others.

In 2012 a super charged cookie was launched by Verizon in the US (well, I say launched, more like sneaked out). This aimed to track Verizon users' web usage without them knowing. To do this, Verizon injected a small amount of code, like a regular cookie, that identifies the person as they visit a website. [3] This was invisible to users and almost impossible to delete. Verizon partnered with Turn, a firm already known for its invention of the zombie cookies that re-spawn immediately once a user tries to delete them.

In her book The Age of Surveillance Capitalism, Shoshana Zuboff describes an interview with Turn's Chief Privacy Officer, who admitted "*We are trying to use the most persistent identifier that we can in order to do what we do*". [4]

According to The Electronic Frontier Foundation - a non-profit organisation for civil liberties online - the Verizon cookie "*...allows third-party advertisers and websites to assemble a deep, permanent profile of visitors' web browsing habits with out their consent.*" [5] In 2016, Verizon was fined $1.3 million by the Federal Communications Commission for their perma-cookie privacy invasion. [6]

The perma-cookie shows how far identity capture, storage and usage can go without a person's knowledge. It exemplifies how a business can possess "*a deep and permanent profile*" of an individual. It also demonstrates how important identity is for targeting ads. And, probably more disturbing than anything else, it goes to show how little a person knows about or has control of their own identity, let alone being able to delete it.

These ad-driven, deeply complex and secretive systems operate unseen in the background of peoples' internet usage and daily lives. In the foreground, however, the internet has often presented another image - one of anonymity. This persuades people that they can behave with absolute freedom from social constraints.

Inspired by anonymity
There is a wide debate about the pros and cons of anonymity online. Some suggest that it is a lifeline for vulnerable groups who need to find support. Others blame it for the internet's wider ills. Many agree that something needs to be done in order to attach accountability to peoples' online behaviour.

The New Statesman writer Sarah Manavis, who specialises in online extremism and social media trends, paints an interesting picture of consumer expectations and the freedom from accountability that has been demanded. *"The early days of the internet were an effective free-for-all, and a decade and a half of social media such as Facebook and Twitter has normalised saying whatever you want, however dangerous or abusive. The principle of free speech has been stretched and mutated to the point where any curbs at all, even on content that would be considered illegal offline, are screamed down as a violation of that right."* [7]

A BBC article about the danger of online anonymity points out the role technology has played in this perceived lack of accountability. *"Technology makes transparency even more important because studies show people are more likely to behave in a dishonest or morally questionable way when they can hide behind it."* [8] And the potential distance involved compounds this issue. David Wasieleski, associate professor of business ethics at Duquesne University in Pittsburgh quoted as saying *"People are less likely to behave badly when their victims are nearby, the web, of course, does a good job of making people feel far away from one another, and thus makes people more likely to attack strangers online who might be on the other side of the globe."* [9]

The online experience of immediate satisfaction without accountability has similarities to the wider landscape of consumer experiences. Little accountability is attached to consumption by a consumer when they can walk away from the litter bin or take no responsibility for the amount of carbon they produce.

There is no acknowledgment of good or bad behaviour as far as high or low impact of consumption is concerned. A person who clocks up 100,000 miles a year in flights bears no responsibility for the carbon they produced from those flights. The only recognition is the "*loyalty*" they have to the airline and the reward comes in the form of air miles, a credit for further flights. A person who spends time and effort avoiding high impact consumption will be left with little more than a clean conscience when they choose the train instead of the plane.

Anonymity is an issue which affects all consumer activities. While the nature of prolific rich consumers can be seen in the brands they choose, the products they consume and the behaviours they reveal, it becomes more difficult when we try to identify the differences between a considerate consumer and a prolific consumer. This becomes impossible when we move that identity, mapping it into a global perspective. For example, comparing a person from a poor region, whose life will be impacted most from climate change and a prolific rich consumer, whose priorities will be very different.

These types of identity comparisons currently have no common system that could capture and compare consumer activity and impact.

Global identity – is this feasible?

The global pandemic of Covid-19 has exposed a big gap in the world's ability to identify a universal identity. Initially, this was difficult when health organisations wanted to track the disease's spread. More recently (2021), discussion has been around the vaccine and a universal vaccine passport system. Even before the Covid-19 Pandemic, international groups were calling for a global identity system. Makhtar Diop, World Bank Vice President for Infrastructure said that *"IDs are taken for granted by those who have them. But lack of identification creates barriers for each individual affected and for the countries they live in."* [10] A report by the World Bank found *"An estimated 1 billion people worldwide do not have basic ID credentials—including as many as 1 in 4 children and youth whose births have never been registered—and many more have IDs that cannot be trusted because they are poor quality or cannot be reliably verified."*

One group of people which has been building consensus around the issue is ID2020. They describe a very different situation from what many people in the West experience. *"For the one in seven people globally who lacks a means to prove their identity, digital ID offers access to vital social services and enables them to exercise their rights as citizens and voters and participate in the modern economy. But doing digital ID right means protecting civil liberties and putting control over personal data back where it belongs…in the hands of the individual."* [11]

They have been working to establish a global identity system since 2016. They advocate *"ethical, privacy-protecting approaches to digital ID."* ID2020 aspire to build this system based on four attributes.

Private: Only you control your own identity, what data is shared and with whom

Portable: Accessible anywhere you happen to be through multiple methods

Persistent: Lives with you from life to death

Personal: Unique to you and you only

There are many complex issues that delay having a global identity system. A major problem is persuading groups who currently have control and influence to agree to share the data and recognise a new system. This will be difficult with businesses (Facebook 2.89 billion active users in 2021)[12] who make money from peoples' data, but might be impossible with countries that perceive a threat in a new global system. Of course, identity is only as good as those who recognise it!

Say cheese

Should governments have control over a person's identity and potentially attach good or bad tags to that data? It depends where a person lives. According to the OECD *"Only 45% of citizens trusted their governments in 2019."* This could be a problem if society and the world are trying to transform consumer behaviour into something more sustainable. The OECD points out that *"Lack of trust compromises the willingness of citizens and business to respond to public policies and contribute to a sustainable economic recovery."*

As pointed out in the last chapter, China is using face recognition a lot to observe the behaviour of its citizens. Experts put this down to different governmental and cultural practices. In a 2020 CNET article, Maya Wang, a senior researcher on China at the Human Rights Watch, describes the difference between national approaches *"It's expressed in a commercial manner in the US, whereas in China it's a state effort,"* Wang said. *"The dynamics are different, and the amount of power is different, but it has striking similarities."* An article by Alfred Ng points out that *"In the US, behavioural engineering can be done through amassing data on people, and pushing or excluding content to them based on predicted personality traits."*[3]

In China the state surveillance system permeates everywhere. It pushes, where other nations nudge. Jaywalking, for example, results in shaming with a photograph on a public monitor and a text message with a fine. But probably even more surprising are the public toilets in one Chinese park that uses face recognition to stop people taking too much toilet roll. Targeting these behavioural improvements doubtless seems petty to people with a democratic country perspective.

In June of 2019, there were hundreds of thousands of people on the streets in Hong Kong protesting the implementation of new Chinese laws to the Hong Kong people. Many of those new laws will infringe on personal rights. The protestors have adopted umbrellas (an icon of earlier 2014 protests), face masks and even laser pointers to target the surveillance cameras. These are new forms of identity protection against modern surveillance.

It is not just China that likes to see their citizens' identities and faces. Many countries have banned face masks for various reasons. In the US some states legislated against wearing masks in the mid twentieth century because they were aiming to halt the violent acts of the Ku Klux Klan.[14] More recently, some European countries have enforced laws against the wearing of masks in public. These masks include motor bike helmets, balaclavas, burqas, niqabs and scarves. Germany has had a ban on disguising a person's identity in public meetings, such as demonstrations, since 1985. The argument is that the police need to be able to identify all participants. Breaking this law can see violators fined, or condemned to spend up to a year in prison.

People in prison awaiting trial in Sweden between 1840 and 1935 wore masks to protect their innocence before appearing in court. This protected their reputations from prejudice in the aftermath of the case.

Branded gravestones

Identity and accountability will need to be associated with the impact of consumption. This needs to be clear, accurate and measurable. Associating a person with a particular brand or specific product can be foggy, transitory and undermine other aspects of their identity, especially in the long term.

We can see examples of this in the way people are memorialised. Augustus Saint-Gaudens, the famous American sculptor of the twentieth century, said the aim in good memorials is "...*to both commemorate greatness and tell complex stories about how the great achieved their mythic status in the public imagination.*"[15] For the rest of us, obituaries and memorials should serve to describe how the departed were perceived by friends and family, with the emphasis on the warmth they brought to the life of others.

These headstones from graveyards for gangster families in Yekaterinburg, Russia, show a potential future of our consumer representations. They have been captured digitally and etched mechanically on to granite. They celebrate the car they drove, the phone they used, the clothes they wore. Commemorating their status through consumer goods could very quickly deteriorate to pastiche over time. What might seem like a cool car, or a contemporary jacket or the latest phone could well deteriorate into hopeless misrepresentation.

Identity and impact together

Over the last couple of centuries, consumers in the richest nations of the world have indulged in increased wealth, product innovation and whole new consumer landscapes. Based on these opportunities, they have learnt a sophisticated language of how to reflect their identity through the things they buy. This behaviour has shifted over time from simply purchasing products packaged with images of desirable scenes to glamorising a whole consumer lifestyle on social media as an "*influencer*".

The location of a person's identity has moved from rudimentary governmental systems to deeply-hidden digital behaviour trackers, creating shadow identities owned by business entities and tyrannical government states.

Across the globe the identity of an individual can vary. In some less developed countries, many people have no formal identity to speak of. As a result, they have little access to basic systems of healthcare and democracy.

This is far from the experience of privileged consumers in rich countries, who can play with identities and lifestyles. They can share this through flattering images, inducing FOMO (fear of missing out) in their followers. For such people, identity is playful and infinitely adaptable. It enables them to overlook consequences and the importance of neutralising the assets of consumption at the end of the lifecycle.

Individual identity will doubtless change over the coming decades. First, increased digitisation will merge consumer data with authoritative civic data and health data. I hope that this might happen with the individual at control in the centre. But that seems unlikely, given the influence of business in managing our data and the enormous value associated with that.

Second, the impact of consumerism on the environment will have to be attached to personal identity. There are few other examples where impact is so disconnected from its specific source. The globalisation of identity will possibly expose the impact on individual consumers and compare the impact of rich consumers against the poor in the process.

What are the potential risks involved in this process? It could be that the celebration of the consumer will change quickly to exposing past behaviour. Future generations, possibly in the midst of natural system collapse, may see the past celebration of brand allegiance as closer to a war crime than something to put on a person's headstone with pride. Identity needs to be attached to the consequences of purchase beyond buying and consuming potential. Hopefully, this is done with sensitivity, reflection and the encouragement of responsibility. It could easily become toxic and shameful.

Legacy number

There are many ways of measuring the impact of consumption over time. Most aren't consumer centric. The majority look only at the material matter of an item and how long it will take to decay in the physical, digital, or service environment. This seems abstract to the consumer who is confronted with legal, environmental, or material time spans.

Measurement needs to relate to the consumer experience and provide context across sectors. One way of representing this would be through a legacy number. This would be contextualised around time to dissipate and the time experienced as a consumer.

Legacy number

A legacy number represents the difference between the length of consumer experience and the length of decay.

Consumer Experience / Decay Time = Legacy Number

Example

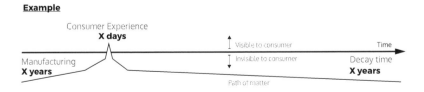

Baked beans

For example, apply this to the act of consuming a tin of baked beans. Product experience duration is recommended at 3-4 days after opening if refrigerated. Product time to decay a tin can in landfill is 50 years according to the Californian State government.[1]

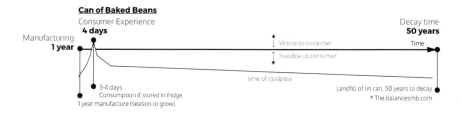

Legacy Number : 1/4562

50 years x 365 = 18250. 18250/4 days = 4562. 1/4562 consumption to landfill.

Dilute lemon

A glass bottle of dilute lemon would provide a different number from a can of beans. This product contents should be consumed within a month after opening. But the length of time for glass to decay in landfill is almost infinite to a million years.[2]

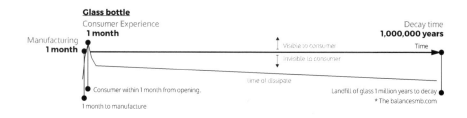

Legacy Number : 1/12000000

1 month x 12. 12 x 1000000 = 12 million. 1/12000000 consumption to landfill.

Flight

The model can stretch across different consumer engagements. For example, a flight between Stockholm and London takes two hours. As a result, loads of carbon dioxide are released into the atmosphere. According to *The Guardian* "...between 65% and 80% of CO_2 released into the air dissolves into the ocean over a period of 20–200years."[3] It takes up to 200 years for most of that to dissipate.

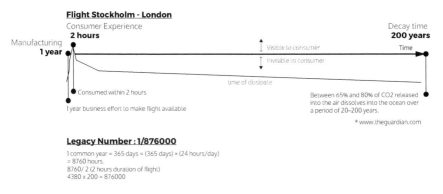

Flight Stockholm - London

Consumer Experience
2 hours

Manufacturing
1 year

Decay time
200 years

Time

Visible to consumer

Invisible to consumer

time of dissipate

Consumed within 2 hours

1 year business effort to make flight available

Between 65% and 80% of CO2 released into the air dissolves into the ocean over a period of 20–200 years.

* www.theguardian.com

Legacy Number : 1/876000

1 common year = 365 days = (365 days) × (24 hours/day)
= 8760 hours.
8760/ 2 (2 hours duration of flight)
4380 x 200 = 876000

Cookie agreement

The model can even be applied to digital experiences. Where a consumer might spend 20 minutes on a website, they might have agreed to cookies on that website that have an expiry date. These can vary greatly. In a recent article I wrote about web cookie expiry dates I found some lasted thousands of years. These were rare, but it was common to find ones that had a duration of over 15 years. [4]

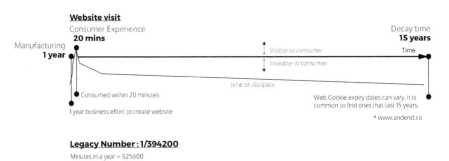

Website visit

Consumer Experience
20 mins

Manufacturing
1 year

Decay time
15 years

Time

Visible to consumer

Invisible to consumer

time of dissipate

Consumed within 20 minutes

1 year business effort to create website

Web Cookie expiry dates can vary. It is common to find ones that last 15 years.

* www.andend.co

Legacy Number : 1/394200

Minutes in a year = 525600
525600 / 20 = 26280
26280 x 15 = 394200

Ends
and
business.

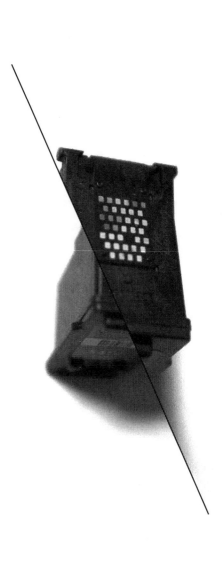

Ch.6

Benefits for business.

All truth passes through three stages: First, it is ridiculed, Second, it is opposed. Third, it is accepted as being self-evident.
Arthur Schopenhauer[1]

Whenever I give a conference talk or present a company workshop, I find that people commonly find it difficult to visualise and think about the end of the consumer lifecycle. It seems to me that people are deeply programmed by the business culture which frames the consumer lifecycle as one of sales and usage. Subsequently, the off-boarding stages appear deeply alien. Which is not surprising, given that we have built a far-reaching consumer society over centuries. It takes time to unshackle minds from that belief.

Over the following pages I shall offer a variety of business arguments that aim to persuade people that the end of the consumer life cycle is a good place to do business.

Consumer satisfaction

Some industries which need to deal with endings as a necessary part of their operation don't always get it right. There are two industries which have had a particular interest in endings over the last decade - the gym industry and the Pay TV industry. Both use contracts which incorporate strict break clauses to dissuade customers from leaving, thus creating an expensive and uncomfortable ending for the consumer.

Let's look at the gym industry first. People - normal people, at least - put on weight over the holidays. Then, thanks to a New Year's resolution to get fit, they sign up with a gym. On average, they go for a few months before slipping back to the way they behaved before, that is, not going to the gym. At which point, the customer says to themselves, *'I am wasting all that money with a gym membership'*. The gym industry has a 30-50% churn according to PT Direct, a personal trainer website.[2]

The gym owners know full well that they need to retain income. So, they get people to sign a fixed term contract which contains punishing break clauses. They believe that this will stop people leaving, which it does, but at what cost! Consumers obviously feel trapped and resign themselves to the pain of going to the gym until the contract is done, or more likely, not going, forfeiting the money and despising the gym company and simply letting the whole attendance that they've paid for lapse.

The Pay TV industry has similar disincentives in its contracts. TV provision is often entwined with other services from the same company, such as internet or phone. So, when you want to leave one of these services, the provider racks up costs on the others to compensate. This looks like a cynical move instead of what should be a pleasant goodbye. An article for the Huffington Post reveals the hidden approaches consumers have experienced. Janna Olson said *"My cable company tried to tell me that if I cancelled the digital service and just got internet and phone service it would cost me more"*.[3] Manuel Briceño revealed a pretty expensive punishment. *"I cut dish (traditional TV) and only use open TV (internet), Netflix, Hulu, Amazon prime video and HBOnow, but now Comcast limited my monthly data to 1,000 gig and if I go over, they charge me 10 dollars for every 50 gig above."* [4]

What these two industries, gyms and Pay TV, have in common is their approach to endings. They are so obsessed with stopping people from leaving that they have allowed the issue to negate any good work done elsewhere. The result is that they actively create negativity about the brand from customers who have left. This chronically limits any chance of re-engagement of the customer over the long term.

What if your business was so comfortable with endings and so confident in the quality of its service that it could make the end of the service a selling point? (Does that sound crazy? I am hoping to convert you over the course of this book) A freedom ending is quite attractive if you have been trapped in the past. Consumers want to have freedom to end their involvement in an amicable way.

According to data by eMarketer, people who have cancelled traditional pay-tv and who are not planning on re-subscribing, grew to 24.9 million by the end of 2017. That was an increase of 43 percent on the previous year. Further shifts in behavior are presented in Deloitte's Digital Trends Survey, that found *"70% of pay-TV subscribers feel they get too little value for their money."* And *"...that 56% of pay-TV customers say they keep their subscription because it's bundled with their home broadband internet"* [5]

Alternatives to bad ends

Netflix wants you to feel comfortable leaving. They say *"We are proud of the no-hassle online cancellation. Members can leave when they want and come back when they want."* [6] Netflix subscriber growth hit 118.9m in 2018, up from 94.36m the previous year. They achieved customer satisfaction of 78%, which dwarfs traditional Pay-TV at 62%, the lowest result in 11 years. [7]

The gym industry has split in half. High-end gyms that offer personal trainers and other services are still doing good business. The middle of the market has collapsed and cheap, low-end gyms, that push easy access and no lock-in periods are dominating. EasyGym is one such gym. They say *"While it will be sad to see you leave, we've made easyGym a no contract gym for a reason. It's flexible so you can join, leave and rejoin whenever you like."*

People like a safe, low risk way out. They want an option of a good ending from a confident company, rather than experiencing entrapment. Creating a good ending doesn't increase the number of people leaving. It just means you care about your customers and how you say goodbye.

Sustainability

Quite rightly, society shouts out its concerns about the environment. Collectively, we want to do our bit, but strategically, are we looking in the wrong places?

I hear many discussions about sustainability in the work I do. Most approaches concentrate on technical improvements in the raw materials used or the manufacturing process. Sometimes such improvements include an aim for circularity in the product lifecycle, reduction of energy costs or leaner processes with better materials. These improvements obviously cover an enormous range of human activities. But what is surprising is the lack of discussion about the consumer experience, which is arguably the core of the problem. Even more noticeably absent is a discussion about the role of marketing, the driver of desire, meaning and emotion in activities relating to consumption. And of course, there is almost no talk about the consumer's experience of the end.

Without the emotional engagement of the consumer at the end there is little incentive for them to move beyond the legal baseline of disposals – the nearest trash bin, the least effort to recycle. Disengagement at the end reinforces a consumer's experience of disposable products that demands no reflection or consideration.

Without the emotional engagement of consumers at the end, businesses who aim to achieve circularity will be trapped sourcing recycled materials from mass collection and reprocessing methods that even now are under strain globally. This fails to achieve a true circular nature between the provider and the consumer.

Unless the consumer engages emotionally at the end, there is little reason for them to take ownership of, or inspire reflection about the long-term consequences of their personal consumption.

Engagement with consumers at the end also helps in off-boarding old products people are hoarding, or don't know how to dispose of. One of the largest growth sectors in US real estate is off-site storage. E-waste – old phones, TVs, computers, etc - is becoming a significant part of this pile of old products. These linger around in our homes, filling up cupboards without the benefit of instructions or destination for disposal. In the US only 17.4 per cent of 2019's e-waste was collected and recycled. These were recoverable materials, valued conservatively at US $57 billion.[8]

According to a piece of research commissioned by the mobile network GiffGaff, as part of their Check your drawers campaign, there is an estimated "55,000,000 *unused mobile phones lying around*" in the UK. In London, people would hoard 13 old gadgets on average – including two mobile phones, two tablets and two laptops, Birmingham came next with 11 pieces of tech, and Southampton with 10 unwanted gadgets.[9]

It is critical to achieve sustainability. The circular economy and cradle-to-cradle approaches are really necessary for chemical, material, and industrial process improvements. But if we don't build on the role of the consumer in the journey towards sustainability, we shall fail to achieve systematic change. We shall continue to fail to stimulate reflection about consumption and have little chance of changing consumer habits.

Emerging legislation

Over the last decade a considerable amount of legislation has been introduced which relates to the end of the consumer lifecycle. Its application can be seen across physical, service and digital product sectors. It has come about largely as a result of businesses creating a culture of overlooked consumer endings. As a result, governments have been forced to act locally, regionally and through joint commitments globally to correct the imbalance in the consumer lifecycle. They improve consumer rights and freedoms around off-boarding. They encourage more awareness about the environmental impact created by consumption.

Below is a selection of examples from across the world.

Right to Repair

Many of the modern devices consumers purchase have restrictions on them to stop the consumer from opening them up and mending them. This happens a lot at the end of the product's life as people try to update a battery or fix a motor. The term Right to Repair has been around for a couple of decades but has only recently been getting traction and becoming law.

US President Joe Biden signed an executive order in July of 2020 called *"Promoting Competition in the American Economy"*.[10] Amongst its wide-ranging policies was a request to the Federal Trade Commission to create rules that stop manufacturers preventing repairs performed by owners and independent repair shops.

The European Parliament made recommendations in 2017 for member states to pass laws giving consumers the Right to Repair. Following this the EU passed laws to force manufacturers to supply parts for repair for up to ten years after manufacture.

France has implemented a repairability score (we will return to this later). Consumers can now see on a scale of 1-10 of how repairable a product is. This score has to be displayed at point of sale. It assesses each product based on 5 criteria – Documentation, Disassembly, Availability of spare parts, Price of spare parts, Product-specific aspects.

The UK currently lags behind France in terms of the consumer experience of mending. It only allows professional repair shops to mend products. Janet Gunter of the Restart Project, who I interviewed in the first Ends book, recently said in a Guardian interview that *"We want to see ecodesign legislation applied to other hard- to-repair tech products and offer the right to repair to everyone."*[11]

Current Account Switch Guarantee

As a result of the fallout of the 2008 banking crisis, the UK government sought to strengthen competition in the banking sector. It commissioned a piece of research from the Independent Commission on Banking. The report revealed that – on average – customers stayed with a bank for 26 years. It also found that 75% of current account holders had never switched banks. One in five people said this was because it was just too difficult to leave.

This difficulty was considered to be a big limiter to increasing openness in markets for the consumer banking sector. As a result, in 2013, the UK government introduced the 7 Day Switch, now called the Current Account Switch Guarantee.[12] The scheme's website describes it thus: *"The Current Account Switch Guarantee means your new bank will switch your payments and transfer your balance, and your old bank will take care of closing your old account. So, you don't need to worry."* Today, in 2021, *"Over 6 million current accounts have been switched so far and more than 40 banks and building societies are already part of the service."* [13]

General Data Protection Regulation (GDPR)

The General Data Protection Regulation was introduced in 2018. It is a European Union data law covering companies and citizens of Europe.[14] Amongst its many sub- laws, it has three clear and empowering laws to allow digital customers to end their data relationships. They are

- The right to data portability
- The right to consent and consent removal
- The right to be forgotten.

Let's consider what these mean in a little more detail.

The right to data portability

Under GDPR,the consumer *"...has the right to obtain from the controller a copy of the provided personal data in an electronic and interoperable format which is commonly used and allows for further use"*. This means a customer of a business can ask that business for the data they hold on them. The customer can then share that data with a competitor business to see if they can provide a better deal.

Many countries already have some legislation around this issue. In the UK, the Data Protection Act and within that, a Subject Access Request, already fulfils this expectation to a degree and allows a person to have access to their data. But it does not define expectations about an 'interoperable format'. This means that the format of that data is in a broadly accepted type, for example Excel.

Some businesses are arguing that the interoperability aspect "...*requires disproportionate effort without consumer lock-in*". This is a somewhat ironic statement, given that 'lock-in' is a characteristic that GDPR attempts to challenge and highlights the mindset that businesses culturally find it hard to deal with endings.

Consent and consent removal

The General Data Protection Regulation (GDPR) states that "*Consent must be clear and distinguishable from other matters and provided in an intelligible and easily accessible form, using clear and plain language*". This promises to be a vast improvement on the current consumer experience! A far more important and, some would say, controversial aspect of the legislation is the expectation that it must be "*as easy to withdraw consent as it is to give it*". This suggests the need for an effective method for consumers to off-board and end their service relationship.

The right to be forgotten

The right to be forgotten "*...entitles the data subject to have the data controller erase his/her personal data, cease further dissemination of the data, and potentially have third parties halt processing of the data.*" If you operate a business involving European citizens' data, they have a right to have their data deleted.

In other words, this law allows any customer of a business to request for their data to be erased. There are a few extreme scenarios where the company can refuse, such as where national security is involved, but in general any European citizen may request this from any business of which they are a customer. Well-organised data businesses have now put the Right to be Forgotten law into a smooth and automated procedure. Anyone who has left Facebook recently might have witnessed this.

The California Consumer Privacy Act (CCPA)

The California Consumer Privacy Act,[15] takes a similar approach to GDPR, aiming to protect the consumer's digital data and embolden their rights online. The original privacy act was established in 1972 aiming to "...*include the right of privacy among the "inalienable" rights of all people*". In 2018 it was updated significantly for the digital age, with the intention of plugging a hole in personal data which they believed formed "...*a breach of security of computerised data that includes personal information*".

The State of California acknowledged that it had led the way in many technological areas, but that its citizens had not seen due progress on their privacy rights. To counter this, the state established five laws to protect its citizens' rights.

1. The right of Californians to know what personal information is being collected about them.

2. The right of Californians to know whether their personal information is sold or disclosed and to whom.

3. The right of Californians to say no to the sale of personal information.

4. The right of Californians to access their personal information.

5. The right of Californians to equal service and price, even if they exercise their privacy rights.[16]

A difference between the CCPA and the European GDPR is that smaller businesses are permitted to be exempt. Small European businesses have found GDPR challenging. The CCPA only requires conformity by California businesses that fall under one of the following criteria.

- Has annual gross revenues in excess of $25 million;

- Buys or sells the personal information of 100,000 or more consumers or households; or

- Earns more than half of its annual revenue from selling consumers' personal information.[17]

Consumer uptake of the CCPA has been reasonably successful. According to a trends report by the American compliance firm DataGrail, "*83% of consumers expect to have control over how businesses use their data, and this research confirms that people are taking action to control their privacy by exercising rights provided by the CCPA*".[18] The report also breaks down consumer requests as follows:

- Consumers opt-out of their personal information being sold most of the time — 48%
- Deletion requests make up 31% of data subject requests
- Access requests make up 21% of data subject requests

Scope 3 emissions

Too many businesses fail to track their customers through the consumer lifecycle to the end. New emissions legislation might change that and inspire businesses to work collaboratively with consumers in the future. Environmental issues could not be more serious. Evidence for climate change is now no longer confined to science papers but to examples in everyday lives. People in Australia are currently (2021) experiencing temperatures of more than 46c (114f). The past four years have seen earth at its hottest.[19] This upward temperature trend will not stop until we reduce greenhouse gas emissions substantially.

To do this, initiatives are underway to work with businesses on emissions improvement. One such initiative is the Greenhouse Gas Protocol. This is a partnership between the World Resources Institute and the World Business Council for Sustainable Development.[20] The Protocol gives sector guidance to businesses covering reporting standards, calculation tools and training. Its three Scopes cover emissions in different parts of any business.

- Scope 1: Direct Greenhouse Gas (GHG) emissions. Covers all greenhouse gas emissions generated by a company - fuel, company vehicles and fugitive emissions (which are emissions of gases or vapours from things like pressurized tank usage).
- Scope 2: Indirect GHG emissions. Consumption of purchased electricity, heat or steam.
- Scope 3: Other indirect GHG emissions. These are upstream activities (goods from providers, business travel, services bought by the business) and downstream activities (distribution of sold products, use of sold products and end of life treatment of sold products).[21]

Various countries are asking their businesses to comply to the Greenhouse Gas Protocol. In the UK for example, businesses already report on Scope 1 & 2 emissions. Reports on Scope 3 are imminent. These are also the trickiest to measure due to their remote location from the business. Two key considerations for Scope 3 are

- The direct use-phase emissions of sold products over their expected lifetime.
- Waste disposal and treatment of products sold by the company at the end of their life.[22]

These considerations are difficult to assess or influence from a distance. To gain an understanding of the consumer's usage of a product requires getting close to it. Many businesses overlook the need to be engaged with the consumer throughout the product lifecycle and even more so with consumer endings. They thus forfeit the opportunity to influence sustainable behaviour. They also lose the ability to capture materials from end-of-life products. Both issues are significant if your business is serious about Scope 3 emissions.

The WEEE Directive

The Waste Electrical & Electronic Equipment Directive (WEEE) is a European law that relates to the disposal of electrical goods such as washing machines, fridges, telephones, TVs, keyboards, etc. According to The Global E-waste Monitor 2020, published by the United Nations University *"In 2019, the world generated a striking 53.6 Million tonnes of e-waste, an average of 7.3 kg per capita. The global generation of e-waste grew by 9.2 Mt since 2014 and is projected to grow to 74.7 Mt by 2030."*[23]

The WEEE Directive aims, at least in the European Union, to set guidelines and targets around the collection, recycling and recovery of electrical products.

At its inception, one of the early intentions was for the *"...creation of collection schemes where consumers return their WEEE free of charge. These schemes aim to increase the recycling of WEEE and/or re-use."*

The success of this intention is debatable, achieving the collection rate in 2017 of *"...47 % in the European Union (measured as the volume of WEEE collected in relation to the average amount of EEE put on the market in the three preceding years, i.e. 2014-2016)."*

Legal complexity

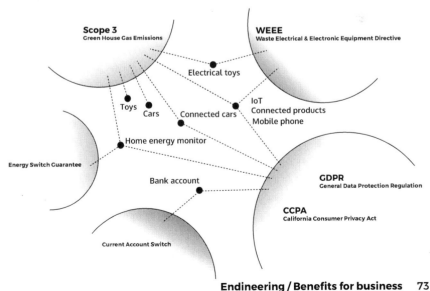

The small selection of legislation examples above demonstrates how much is changing for producers. As consumer desires increase and become more complex, and the products available attempt to stay relevant, the complexity of legal endings gets complicated. A single product like a mobile phone might be affected by three different laws at the end of the consumer experience.

The consumer might well be hit with three different legal experiences. It will be for the provider to make these experience coherent and meaningful.

Innovation

Innovation is a term which has frequently been overused by business. It has been applied – in a rather casual way - to subtle and marginal changes. Real innovation requires seismic shifts in vision. This is something that Peter Drucker, the famous management consultant, endorsed. He called for businesses to rethink the products, markets and services they offer every three years by asking the question *"If we were not in it already, would we be going into it now?"* He called this method systematic abandonment.[24]

Just imagine that there is a part of the consumer lifecycle that lots of businesses overlook. They do this to such a degree and have been doing so for such a long time, that it seems alien to even consider any alternative. Now imagine how little work has been done in this area and what opportunities are there.

To start rethinking endings as an innovation issue, let's look at two areas that are wide open in terms of opportunity.

Engagement cycle
Business models are changing. Consumers don't stay with one brand forever. They move between brands, embracing mobility in the modern marketplace. Customers enjoy the benefits of faster account creation, more convenient payment mechanisms and delivery times counted in minutes. Very few customers are really new to any market nowadays.

Loyalty isn't the bond many assume. Byron Sharp, in his book How Brands Grow, argues that many people buy out of habit, not loyalty. *"Loyalty is everywhere but it's seldom exclusive – buyers purchase more than one brand, and the more purchases an individual makes the more brands he or she buys. Polygamous or divided loyalty is quite the norm. So, no brand should expect its buyers to be 100% loyal."*[25]

Business innovation has been focused around the on-boarding and usage experience. They overlook the need for a business to offer the consumer a good off-boarding experience. This results in a proliferation of cliff edges where the consumer experience drops off suddenly when the end happens.

In this fallout, assets are lost, responsibility is shunned and opportunity for long term engagement disappears. We can define this approach as a single engagement model. This is where a business is structured around a single engagement of sales, onboarding and usage.

The problem with the single engagement model is that ends happen, come what may. Everything comes to an end, and so will the engagement a business has created with a consumer. When the end happens, shards of broken experiences break off. These fragments then linger in the physical, service or digital environments. Examples of such broken shards of experience are the plastics in the sea. They are resources a company failed to keep within the consumer lifecycle so as to be able to reclaim them in a controlled way. Or they may be the lingering images that a consumer was encouraged to share online by a company that failed to design a way to un-share those assets. They might also be a financial product, like a pension, that someone created decades ago, but is now lost because the company failed to create an ending that would last for the length of a career, life or marriage. Opportunities lie in moving away from a single engagement model towards a world that imagines and innovates around the end stage.

Single Engagement

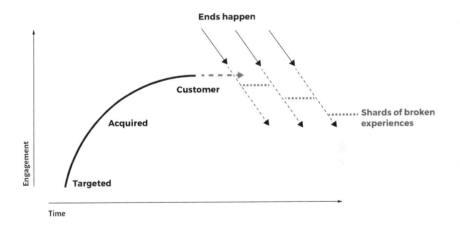

Multiple engagement

The best of future businesses will look at the ending as part of a longer strategy. This would be one that considers a customer's situation across multiple engagements. These may be scattered over years, maybe even decades. In such a case a business needs to consider itself a multiple engagement provider. It would take the off- boarding as seriously as the on-boarding.

Multiple Engagement

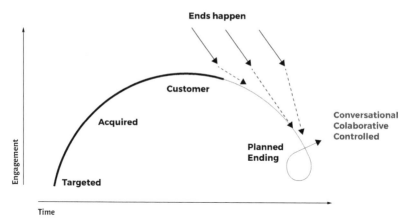

Much of current marketing can be broken into short term and long-term plans. A short-term plan considers tactical issues, matters such as engagement on differing channels, price changes or promotional activities. Long term plans might consider economic, consumer, and market trends.

At off-boarding emotional messages would be sent that engaged the consumer right up to departure and build in long-term meaning and brand equity for the business. This will help encourage collaborative efforts around sustainability, reclaiming assets in a controlled way and establishing a responsible partnership in the long term.

Creating a memory

The second area that shows an enormous potential opportunity is the creation of long-term memory in the consumer experience. By the end of the consumer relationship, a lot of the original meaningful communication has been lost. The consumer often experiences the off-boarding of a product independently from the provider. Their personal perception is rich and meaningful, even if it is not satisfactory or enjoyable. This ending has a significant impact on memory.

Peak End rule is the process of creating memories from two points. Described by Daniel Kaheman,[26] it suggests there are two moments of influence that create memories - the peak and the end (more about this in the 'How should it feel' chapter). For a business it ideally means having a really good product experience within the consumer lifecycle and being present at the end to embed the best memories. But this is, of course, impossible if the business has already left the consumer experience behind. This leaves the end out of control. In essence, the business loses fifty percent of memory to chance. This is an enormous risk.

Businesses spend a great deal of money building brand equity through advertising and marketing. Not all of this money ends up with customers, or even potential customers. Yet it has been spent. Imagine having a significant influence on people who are already your customers and will carry personal endorsements to other people after they leave – they are the most trusted type of customer. Now think how much equity is lost failing to create good memories at the end of the lifecycle.

Bias tools limit thinking

Some of the tools used by businesses create an unhealthy bias at the end of the consumer lifecycle. This bias can frame a business's thinking, bend business ethics, risks brand perception over the long term and limits strategic direction.

Brand principles

Many businesses proudly portray their brand principles elsewhere in the consumer lifecycle but see them dissolve quickly at off-boarding.

It is common to see characteristics like honesty, transparency and pride in a business's brand guidelines. These ethics will then be reinforced at on-boarding through marketing messages for the customer. They are often repeated throughout the following engagements. But these principles will be bent at off-boarding to halt the customer's departure. It is common at this point to see manipulative behaviour, with hard sales tactics being used.

Predicting endings

Predictive analytics software[27] can serve as an impressive predictor of the end. It is a growing market, predicted (sorry about the pun) to grow to $21.5 billion by 2025. [28] It can be used in a variety of ways to gain insights into current customers or to assess new markets. For example, insurance companies might use them to do risk assessments. Marketing might use them to find new customers. But they are also used to predict customer churn – endings.

A business will consider a customer as "*churned*" after the period since they last engaged with the company or product has elapsed. The cost of churn is not only the loss of that customer, but is also the marketing cost of acquiring a new customer to replace them. The ideal scenario is to predict that a customer is leaving and then to stop them before they do. As you can probably imagine, that is a very useful tool to a business.

Optimove is one of many businesses selling these types of products. They describe the process of predicting churn as "*modelling precise customer behaviours and attributes which signal the risk and timing of customer churn.*" One of their approaches is Targeted Proactive Retention, which means "*knowing in advance which marketing action will be the most effective for each and every customer.*" They claim that this is "*based on combining customer churn prediction and marketing action optimisation.*" [29]

What is apparent in many of these predictive churn tools, and in fact the culture around them, is how binary the assumptions are. For example, it is assumed that there are only two scenarios.

- 1. The customer leaves - which is bad.
- 2. The customer stays - which is good.

Heart framework

The bias described above extends to other tools in product development. For example, a popular methodology in software development is the HEART framework from Google.[30] It stands for Happiness, Engagement, Adoption, Retention and Task Success. Product teams measure success using these dimensions, but this only works well if you are measuring the success of someone staying with the service. An off- boarding experience can't be measured positively using the bias factors of the HEART framework. Using tools like this obviously influences employees' attitudes towards off-boarding, particularly if employee goals or bonuses are linked to HEART framework metrics.

Better tools

Tools used by businesses will need to become more aware and nuanced at off- boarding, especially as new laws demand deeper knowledge at the end of product life. For example, Scope 3 greenhouse gas emission laws will make the gathering of knowledge at the product end of life critical. Businesses will need to know the emissions of that product's final moments. It's sadly apparent that very few businesses know even roughly what happens to their product after a sale. Just creating basic feedback mechanisms and data sources will be a massive effort for many.

Using tools properly by businesses can establish deeply held beliefs and practices. Over time it will become increasingly important to build knowledge and inspire discussion about consumer off-boarding experiences. This will help businesses to fulfil their brand principles in the long term as customers come and go. It will help widen ideas about customer experience.

The consumer experience of consequences

There is a long drawn-out sequence, often occurring over decades, of people dealing with human-made problems. It plods from scientific awareness to government legislation to business acceptance and finally - a consumer experience. History is littered with businesses who have tried to prevent their customers from recognising the role they have in the consequences of consumerism.

Processing these issues can be hard. It might take some time for full knowledge to emerge. But once it has, businesses should be clear in their actions. They should initiate open, collaborative discussion as part of the consumer experience. This should provide the consumer with actionable ways to counter negative consequences.

Smoking

One of the familiar stories of hidden consequences relates to the smoking industry. It was nearly a hundred years ago (in 1929) that Fritz Lickint of Dresden in Germany[31] published a paper, based on statistical evidence, showing a link between tobacco and lung cancer. It was overlooked, or maybe avoided, and it wasn't until 1954 that doctors in the UK started to make similar connections. And it even took another 10 years before US doctors came to a slow realisation that smoking isn't good for humans.

It took another 20 years for the UK government to start raising this issue with consumers. It introduced warnings on cigarette packaging in 1971. They printed *"WARNING by H.M. Government, SMOKING CAN DAMAGE YOUR HEALTH"*[32] in cold black on white text, in a sans serif font, down the left hand side of the box. This was a most un-engaging contrast to the rich emotional messages that tobacco companies were using to sell their product: a large on-boarding and off-boarding discrepancy.

It wasn't until May 2016 that the UK launched Plain packaging legislation. This forbade any positive, branded messages about the consumption of the product. And at the same time, it mandated drab dark brown coloured packaging, specific pack shapes and the font Helvetica at 14 point for the brand name.

These actions did away with the emotional messages about the product benefit and the ultimate consequences. Could the smoking industry have engaged earlier and communicated the issue with the consumer, then potentially more lives would have been saved.

Obesity

A trend in weight increase started to develop in the US in the early 1970s. According to the Lancet this trend came about through a *"...rapid increase in food production and thus an increase in food portion sizes; accelerated marketing, availability, and affordability of energy dense foods; and widespread introduction of cheap and potent sweetening agents, such as high-fructose corn syrup, which infiltrated the food system and affected the whole population simultaneously."*[33]

Obesity has been growing across the globe. Government acknowledgment

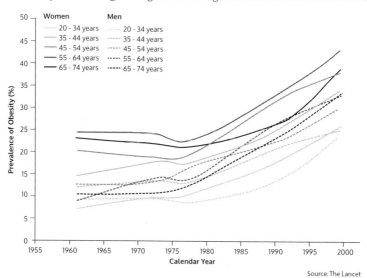

Source: The Lancet

of, and action to deal with the growing obesity crisis, varies between countries. Earlier initiatives included marketing bans for TV adverts of junk food. More recently, in 2013 the UK government introduced the traffic lights scheme.[34] This was rolled out slowly across Europe. It required a clear indication of the quantities of sugar, salt, fat in a food product. This helped people to make a quick judgement about whether or not to consume it.

Some of the companies that have been criticised as fuelling the obesity crisis have adjusted their product lines, marketing and even whole businesses to counter the issue. They have attempted to help customers make better decisions.

In 2009 PepsiCo said in its Annual Report that it was "...*committed to delivering sustainable growth by investing in a healthier future for people and our planet,*"[35] This was followed by adjustments to PepsiCo's products, reducing fat and sugars and helping people manage their consumption by detailing calorie-specific serving sizes. They recognised the end/ultimate consequence of consumption and they acknowledged it. They have acted on it. They have visualised it to the consumer. This has helped them to reflect upon it and put counter-measures into effect, thus helping consumers to reach balanced conclusions around their consumption. An appropriate ending!

Aviation

The first Intergovernmental Panel on Climate Change was established in 1988. The subject was a niche issue back then. Awareness was slow to build, but evidence has been building. It is now deafening. Industries have been called upon to help change this. It was ascertained that consumer behaviour was one of the key factors that needed to adapt. Some industries have performed better than others.

The aviation industry as a whole, has been disappointingly late to react. It has escaped regulation until relatively recently. It was only in January of 2018 that the industry was brought under one initiative –CORSIA - Carbon Offsetting and Reduction Scheme for International Aviation. This saw 70 countries (around 85% of international aviation activity) volunteer to participate in the scheme.[36]

Experiencing the end

In the aviation industry progress has been slow and the consumer experience of the emissions generated by airplanes has become invisible. A few years ago, many ticket purchases on airline websites would include an opportunity to off-set carbon. It would show the amount of carbon released as a result of the traveler's flight and recommend countering that by planting trees. It was directly actionable by the consumer. Airlines now only seem to mention this in the context of the company's green credentials.

This lack of acknowledgment is comparable to the smoking industry's approach to the ill effects of smoking. It's not that the airline industry is denying climate change, or even not doing anything about it. But currently it offers a complicit relationship of denial.

We all know that flying is bad for the environment. We all know we should probably fly less. We need to acknowledge that in the consumer relationship. This would provide a safe, transparent place where the problems of climate change are measured, acknowledged, reflected upon and actioned in a consumer/provider partnership.

A good place to start would be shutting down air miles schemes before they become evidence in this denial. They celebrate the activity but many fail to provide opportunities for people to reflect on or counter the issue.

Retirement village

An old friend contacted me recently and thought I would find their story of designing for the ending experience at a retirement village interesting. Retirement villages are a growing sector. The process of moving into one is smooth. But the process of ending the relationship can be traumatic, emotional and can often be devastating to vulnerable people and their families. Alex Crowfoot picks up the description from here.

Background

"The company had already completed some research and identified a number of issues. While residents love life in the retirement village, the process of leaving was causing a lot of problems - it was bureaucratic, inflexible, and hard to navigate.

Residents mainly leave because they are going into aged care. Some choose to move nearer to their family, and some residents pass away. In each case, people are stressed. No-one knows what to expect from the process and the families are often heavily involved in something very alien to them.

At on-boarding, when people move into a retirement village, they usually sign a leasehold. Part of the deal is that they defer some costs and fees until they leave so they can have a better lifestyle while they are there. That's all very clear in the contract you sign when you enter the village, but you can't know how much you will pay because you don't know how long you'll live there. They don't know the end upfront. All of which leaves a lot to be resolved at the end. Also in the contract is that you'll have to, at a minimum, share the cost of restoring the unit to a saleable condition, which typically costs tens of thousands of Australian dollars. There are many further complexities, for example a hot residential market doesn't mean a hot retirement village market, but sellers expect them to be the same.

The current process of leaving:

· The resident/family inform the company the unit will be vacated
· The company inspect the unit, determine its renovated value, decide what needs to be done and get quotes
· The resident/family receive a letter with the valuation, a rough estimate of the money they might get if a certain sale price is achieved, and a summary of deductions including renovation costs
· They agree to or dispute the renovation cost and valuation
· Renovation, etc is done to the unit once it's empty
· The unit goes on the market
· The family get money once sold

Particular issues

· The property company controls the whole leaving process - valuation, renovation, sale of the unit. It's all highly regulated and above board but it makes residents and families feel suspicious.
· The company only makes money from the sale of the property, not the renovation, but families don't know this. The residents and families can feel suspicious about the amount of work proposed.
· Families have no idea what their parent signed up to.
· There is a high degree of stress as often the family need the money from the sale to pay for aged care, which needs an upfront lump sum.
· The property company inspect the property almost immediately after notification of "exit", which comes across as insensitive.

In essence, the process was messy, business led, bureaucratic, riddled with issues.

Working closely with the company, we:

· Visualised the process for residents and families so they understood what was to come and added informative

resources for people who are most likely experiencing death of a parent or moving a parent to aged care for the first time
· Discovered data that could be used to trigger communications so that the family could be informed where things were up to without adding to workload
· Identified numerous opportunities to humanise communications, whether through use of language or removal of things that simply hadn't been thought about in terms of impact

The new ending

Found a way to offer more choice to residents and/or their families rather than having no choice
Realised that if the renovations could be done after a new purchaser was found, then we could
· 1) for families: prevent them having to deal with renovations at all
· 2) for the business: avoid all the delays that occur when families have to approve renovations or worse, dispute them
· 3) for the business and for new residents: offering new residents the ability to tailor the renovation to what they want before they move in. This prevented the waste that occurred when new residents would move in and make changes, like rip out a brand-new carpet to put in wooden floorboards. Now, they will make that choice before the work is done. We also saw some opportunities to offer sustainability upgrade packages to incoming residents, like solar, grey water recycling, water tanks.

By improving the consumer ending we increased control and reduced stress for the people leaving. Making a far more pleasant experience. But we also found an entirely new market proposition for the property company, and more choice for people moving into retirement units."

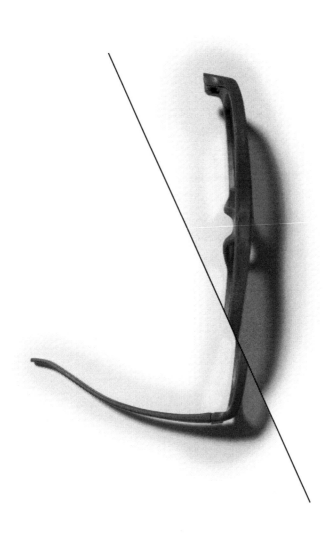

Ch.7

ROI of ends.

A common question that I get asked is *'What would the return on investment (ROI) be of ends?'* Investing in better consumer off-boarding cannot be considered in isolation. It needs to be located in the wider context of changing consumer awareness, emerging legislation, marketing trends and other investments. To answer it, I want to break down the question into separate, more specific issues.

- What is the potential cost of creating consumer off-boarding experiences?
- Where is the investment growth from consumer experience coming from?
- How can we put a value on consumer experience at the end of the consumer lifecycle?

What is the potential cost of creating consumer off-boarding experiences?

There is a cost to engaging more actively in consumer off-boarding. It will have financial and time consequences for businesses. Teams will need to be trained. Changes to approach, communication, logistics and even culture will need to happen. For some sectors, especially physical product producers, costs may be higher as they implement far-reaching changes to customer engagement alongside sustainability, databases and logistics. For others it will mean simple changes, some empathy, training and extending the company focus. In the following passage I shall point out some of the key elements that I think will require investment. Much of this will be on a general level because I can't talk about the specifics of your individual businesses. Readers should consider the following as a starting point for further investigation.

Business culture change

Many businesses are trapped in a single engagement model. They see their business in terms of one sales cycle. Moving business culture from single engagement thinking to a broader view with multiple engagements, potentially over decades, is going to be a challenge for some. This cultural attitude about the consumer lifecycle is deep-seated. It has been established thinking in business schools for decades and is well-established boardroom normality. But a shift has been happening. Now, through consumer pressure, it is common for a business to have a sustainability strategy. Continued momentum in this direction may see companies go beyond the issues of sustainable manufacturing and materials to creating consumer experiences that support a better ending.

Skills

The main requirement for delivering richer experiences at off-boarding would be making allowance for the costs of increased communication and interaction with the consumer. The skill sets needed to create these types of experience are often available in marketing, product and design teams. Their roles will need to expand.

Marketing teams, for example, will need to go beyond what's needed to ensure retention and become positively engaged in the ending of the consumer experience. They will need to scale up their vision from a single sale, to creating brand equity over many sale cycles. They need to have off-boarding experiences as a key element of that responsibility so as to build meaning, direction and a consumer-provider partnership. More extensive necessities will no doubt be required. For example, the development of a company voice to be heard at the end of the product's life might take time and investment.

Product and design teams will need to consider the off-boarding as well as the on-boarding experience. Some, no doubt, have already been engaging with sustainable approaches to their physical products. That's great. Building experiences on top of functional and material benefits will work well and maximise emotional meaning for the consumer at off-boarding. Building capability alongside previous efforts is a rational and clear-sighted investment.

For teams working on products with less of a physical impact, investment might be less. Off-boarding might be simpler, without the need to reclaim materials. The least costly investments would probably be for purely digital products, as they are potentially as simple as some new processes in data management and deletion. Revealing these would generate a clear, actionable and branded experience for the consumer. Such a process would come as an extension to ongoing product development. The cost would be mainly an investment in staff and time. It might even create a need for new roles for people who specialise in these issues.

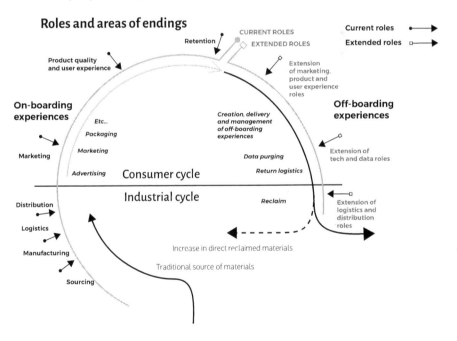

Roles and areas of endings

CURRENT ROLES ◆ — ►
Current roles ●——►
EXTENDED ROLES ◇
Extended roles ▭——►

Retention
Product quality and user experience
Extension of marketing, product and user experience roles

On-boarding experiences
Off-boarding experiences

Etc...
Creation, delivery and management of off-boarding experiences

Packaging
Marketing
Marketing
Advertising
Data purging
Extension of tech and data roles

Return logistics

Consumer cycle
Industrial cycle
Reclaim
Extension of logistics and distribution roles

Distribution
Logistics
Manufacturing
Sourcing

Increase in direct reclaimed materials
Traditional source of materials

Research and measurement

For many companies researching the off-boarding experience will not be easy. Unlike interactions with current active customers, where communication channels might be rich and measurement tools plentiful, the end of the consumer life cycle is not as well served.

Qualitative measuring tools such as reviews, exit interviews and Net

Promoter Score are good. But these tend to focus on the product offering.

Quantitative tools are used within the consumer lifecycle, especially with products that have a digital aspect, produce rich and plentiful data. This drops off quickly once the consumer has left. Building research and measurement capability will be difficult and time consuming but might not be the costliest phase.

Aligning with legislation

In recent decades there has been an increase in legislation around the end of the product lifecycle. Businesses will be expected to abide by environmental, financial, data, health and safety rules. Some of these are particularly relevant at consumer off- boarding. For example, cleaning up and deleting data under GDPR or tracking end of life for products under Scope 3 Green House Gas Emissions, which we heard about in the Benefits for Business chapter.

Industry has invested a great deal in adhering to these new rules. As a consumer experience, legislation is often invisible. It's often pushed behind the scenes, out of sight. This might not always have been the best approach. Encouraging consumers to understand the legislation will help businesses to become more compliant and create bonding in responsibility. We can see evidence in the success of this with recently introduced data legislation, with GDPR and The California Consumer Privacy Act (CCPA). Businesses are getting much better at communicating compliance with legislation as part of the consumer experience.

Lifting compliance to a level of consumer experience and helping to build bonding and common purpose between consumer and provider will be beneficial to many companies. It may even result in reducing the costs of compliance and increasing consumer engagement with legislation.

Logistics, assets, communication touchpoints

Building logistic capability for end of product life is no small undertaking. Experiences built alongside can help provide meaning for, and engagement with the consumer. Investment will be needed to align these initiatives.

To reclaim materials directly from the consumer will necessitate the extension of the normal logistics used in shipping or usage. For example, if a producer wanted to retrieve a bike at end of product life, a system of identification would need to be included on the product at manufacture. The consumer could then use this at off- boarding. This process would require a database that identified historic products with a location. That would then kick start a process of logistics which would send packaging to the consumer for them to return the item. This would require expansion in logistics, shipping and the design of packaging. All these pile up to a significant investment. But this is not an unsurmountable task. In fact, the fashion industry has been making good progress here.

Businesses with less physical products might still need to consider longer term relationships if those products have significant carbon impact. They still might require communication with consumers to ensure carbon impact is neutralised. For example, the long term impact of a flight might require communication between company and consumer long after the trip has finished. The company could update the consumer with details of how to neutralise the lingering carbon assets. Investment will be required to finance digital communication with the individuals.

Building richer consumer experiences around end of life will require more communication assets. This investment could be an extension of an established communication budget. For example, the marketing team might need to produce more assets, packaging, adverts and information to guide and engage the consumer.

First steps, achievable budgets

The costs above reflect an ideal level of engagement for consumer off-boarding across different sectors. Within this it assumes that a period of investigation and due diligence would have taken place and that the business is committed to deliver on that vision. Before that ideal level of investment, there should be a potential first step that would be a minimal cost to any business. The outcome of this would define a path for further investigations, with specifics for individual businesses.

A first step project of this nature could be done in-house. It would require either an individual or team with significant access to knowledgeable people in the organisation to assemble a plan. This would be a minimal investment, depending on the size of the business. It could be accomplished in an afternoon for a small business or within a month for a larger one.

Where is the growth of consumer experience coming from?

Businesses are growing their investment in consumer experience as a vehicle for increasing engagement with products, pushing profits, innovation and efficiencies. According to Forbes,

- Companies with a customer experience mindset drive revenue 4-8% higher than the rest of their industries.

- Two-thirds of companies compete on customer experience, up from just 36% in 2010.

- Companies that lead in customer experience outperform laggards by nearly 80%.

- 84% of companies that work to improve their customer experience report an increase in their revenue.

- 73% of companies with above-average customer experience perform better financially than their competitors.[1]

As a longtime advocate of the customer experience, it's great for me to see interest in it increasing, despite most attention going towards the on-boarding and usage phases. This interest will widen the remit of the discipline, no doubt expanding it to other areas beyond core functionality. Endings will start to be considered as an important part of the process of dealing with consumers. This is a growing field. There is significant appetite for taking on-board new areas of the consumer experience discipline.

Alongside this increase in direct investment in consumer experience, there is an adjacent area of concern about considerate consumerism. Nielsen, the data analytics firm, found that *"A new era of sustainability is rising. Consumers in markets big and small are increasingly motivated to be more environmentally conscious and are exercising their power and voice through the products they buy."*[2] They found *"...a whopping 81% of global respondents feel strongly that companies should help improve the environment."*

Engagement in this area is often interpreted simply as consumers purchasing products that are better for the environment. But significant improvements can come from the way people dispose of their products as well. Endings form a bridge between consumption and actionable improvements consumerism.

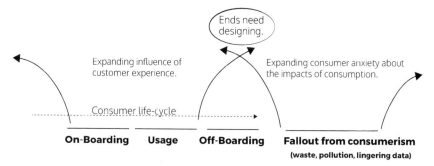

How can we put a value on consumer experience at the end of the consumer lifecycle?

Some say that consumer experience needs to demonstrate its value, arguing that it can occasionally be considered as an indulgence, neither practical nor profitable. Certainly, ends are perceived as such for many people. And I understand their logic, but with fresh thinking there are clear benefits for businesses to engage in the way people leave a consumer relationship.

To consider the business case for ends, I want to look at a piece of work by KPMG that models the value of investing in customer experience. They say *"Capital investments and operating costs to provide these experiences will continue to climb. To be effective and invest wisely, organizations need to gain a thorough understanding of Customer Experience (CX) Journey Economics"* [3]

KPMG's CX Journey Economics aims to illustrate where the balance lies between what sort of experience is expected by the consumer and how much money a company could invest in that customer experience. This provides a useful basis for looking at the value of investing at the end of the consumer lifecycle.

KPMG focus

"We recommend linking investments designed to repair experience shortfalls to specific customer activity measures such as attrition, repurchase rates and/or customer lifetime value. Such measures can then be translated into a financial impact."

Companies such as KPMG see the benefits of customer experience being focused on the acquisition and usage periods of the consumer lifecycle. The best of modern businesses, however, are considering external aspects far more as part of their wider responsibilities. These responsibilities can't stay unseen in factory efficiencies, or product material improvement. The consumer experience needs to be part of a sustainable future. Consumer representatives, legislation, and governments are all expecting more responsibility from companies. The most fruitful new areas will be expanding that focus to be experience-based. Improving off-boarding interfaces and methods of product disposal, deletion and returning items, are all good examples of off-boarding experiences.

Cost of the impact

The change in attitudes towards frequent flyer programs is a very good example of the consumer experience being expanded beyond the initial

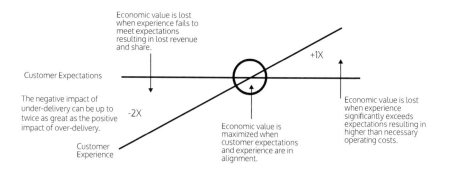

intention of the product. Once an accolade to be proud of, Air Miles are now considered to mark negatively against a person's social responsibility. It is clear that the balance of customer experience with something like Air Miles has eroded over time.

Value in consumer experience investment can't be a snap shot. An updated version of the KPMG model that represents the long-term risks might look like this. It shows an experience that fades over time. The consumer experience has a lingering shadow that exposes the negative aspects of the engagement. It also exposes the business to an unmitigated risk.

This reveals a tangible target for investment at the end of the consumer experience and a legitimate purpose – to halt the erosion of the desired consumer experience over time.

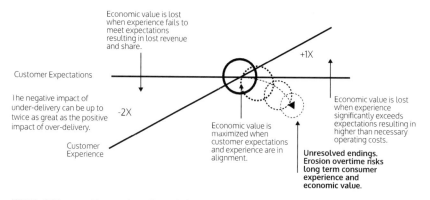

KPMG: CX Journey Economics + Unended CX risks economic value

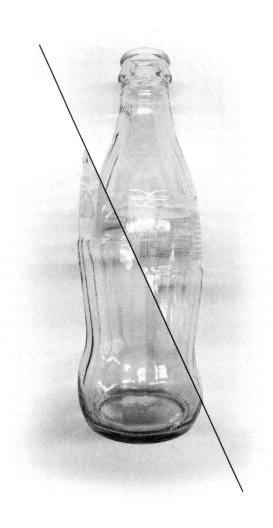

3 Denmark:
A Beautiful Exit.

Mobile phone companies are usually known for their hard-nosed retention tactics. Such tactics are evident in the long-winded processes involved in leaving a service. This often requires lengthy periods of communication with a call centre. 3 Denmark took a different approach. Questioning that established thinking, they started to look for a better ending.

This story starts with the 3 Denmark customer support team. They were the people who approved a customer leaving or talked them around to staying. They had worked tirelessly on other areas of efficiency in every aspect of their customer support department. But the last priority was to look at improving the customer leaving experience. Until that point, this was one of the most time consuming activities for the team. This task now came under scrutiny and

required improvement.

Two people were key in this investigation for 3 Denmark and shared their story with me. Louise Klemens, a product owner, and Soren Hartvig Laursen, a UX designer for the Beautiful Exit project.

First, they started looking at the Danish competitor landscape of endings for telecoms customers. None of the major players had a smooth positive ending in place. All were still operating a restricted exit strategy. This was awash with dark patterns and dead ends for the consumer. So, there was an obvious market opportunity.

There was also a brand argument, as the company had adopted 'transparency' as one of its key brand attributes. The team felt it was important that this was reflected everywhere in the consumer experience of the company and having a smooth and clear ending worked well to reinforce that. Personally, I find this very encouraging. Too few companies hold themselves accountable to the brand promise at off-boarding in the same way as they do for on-boarding.

Obviously, there were doubts on the business side, as you can imagine, with any business which has decades of doing something in a particular way. And especially for an issue as culturally significant as making it easy for customers to leave. There was a lot of anxiety. But the team was highly trusted. They had carried out their due diligence and had put together a strong argument for better consumer endings.

The solution would be placed inside 3 Denmark's current customer app. This is easily accessible through the 'My 3' area, which is where other account functionality is found by customers. The off-boarding flow is entirely digital which reduces the load on the customer support team. There would not be any offer upgrades or special persuasion to keep a customer anymore. It was a clear, honest, transparent solution for the business and the consumer alike.

At launch everyone was watching customer numbers very closely. They were worrying that people were going to leave en masse. Over hours and days, there was a lot of attention on the project. But you know what? Not much changed. There wasn't the exodus that retention-crazed fearmongers might have us all believe when creating an ending. No more people left 3 Denmark because it was easier.

It was great to talk to Louise and Soren. They delivered an ending that reinforced the brand values, reduced the load on the customer service team, saved the business money and increased the customer experience at a critical point. Now the team sees other opportunities with endings beyond this first brave step.

Ch.8

Benevolent beginnings -are they enough?

Charity is said to begin at home, but it might be more accurate to say that it begins with a sale. It's often at the point of purchase that a consumer finds it easiest to behave benevolently. By purchasing something, they can endorse themes like better working conditions, or healthier growing methods for food, or sustainable material usage or thousands of other well-deserving issues. These issues are communicated to them expertly using sophisticated marketing techniques. Many of these techniques have been established for decades, some even for centuries, and have been very successful at changing behaviours in the consumer, in businesses, in government and in international trade.

Examining this issue isn't intended to criticise the good intentions of people and organisations who are trying to improve the world. They have certainly made the world a better place. But it is to question objectively whether we focus overly much on improving the on-boarding and purchase experience, while the ending, and ultimate consequence of consumption is overlooked. It might demonstrate just how deeply the bias of starting a consumer experience overshadows the proper and responsible ending of one.

To consider this issue we will look at the history of some themes which have developed as part of the purchase experience and how they have matured into marketing campaigns. We will also look at some of the impacts of consumption and consider how creating similarly benevolent off- boarding experiences has not happened.

Early organics

As far back as the 1900s, Sir Albert Howard, Rudolf Steiner and F. H. King[1] were starting to develop organic growing techniques. They were concerned about human-manufactured pest controls. They were becoming early champions of organic approaches in horticulture in their respective countries - Britain, Switzerland, and the United States. They believed that such approaches promised a better route to healthier crops.

Over the following decades interest in organic farming grew alongside wider consumer concerns. J.I. Rodale and his son Robert published Organic Gardening and Farming magazine in 1940.

A little later Rachel Carson's Silent Spring, published in 1962[2], stimulated fear of, and an awakening to the issue in the general public. It documented the damage inflicted on the food chain by synthetic pesticides. The book's impact was felt widely, igniting changes across food production and farming. Interest in, and sales of organic food have been increasing ever since, particularly through the 21st century. There are now organic options for almost any food. Sales in the US increased from $20 billion in 2008 to $45 billion in 2017.[3]

As a consumer experience, there is a lot of detail that goes into the origin of organic produce. It has been necessary to establish clear regulation at country and international levels. Legitimately produced and labelled goods are easily recognised, helping consumers to trust the authenticity of organic products.

Beyond the factual details about a product - chemical impact, regulation - the story that the consumer gets told is that the product is part of a wider lifestyle choice. This powerful story is assembled, drawing on a variety of issues and contexts, which build meaning and emotion into each step. The climax of the story is the point which culminates in the moment of consumption. In contrast, there are few choices about what happens after organic food has been consumed. Consumers are not informed about the residue, the destination or the importance of waste. This is well established and is invisible to people in rich nations. Yet, as we will see later in this chapter, the outcomes of our bodily movements through toilets and sewage could be considered equally to the source of our food and water. Could these stories be linked in a universal full food lifecycle campaign? I doubt many have the stomach for it.

Fair trade

There is a similar pattern with social issues being promoted benevolently to consumers at the start of the consumer lifecycle. Fair Trade is now something we are all being invited to consider when purchasing goods. Fair Trade principles go back centuries. The earliest evidence was demonstrated in pre-capitalist Europe, when religious groups would champion an improved moral agenda.

More recently, in 1827, Thomas M'Clintock, a Quaker, founded the Free Produce Society[4]. It aimed to discourage and boycott slave-based goods. It championed the value of the honest labour of free men and women. The theme grew and in 1838 a number of organisations came together to form the American Free Produce Association. They encouraged people to seek non-slave-produced alternatives rather than products from slave owners. It published pamphlets and the journal Non- Slaveholder, alongside building non-slave product distribution channels. It failed due to the extra financial costs of "*free produce*" which were always higher than competing slave-made goods.

After the Second World War, two initiatives, one from Mennonite Central Committee (MCC) and a second from SERRV International (Sales Exchange for Refugee Rehabilitation and Vocation)[5] offered steps towards what we see today. Both established Fair Trade supply chains to sell handicrafts made in developing countries. These were then shipped to charity shops and ethnic stores in the US and Europe. Before the nineteen eighties this industry sold few agricultural goods. Then demand for handicrafts started to soften and at the same time, commodity prices dropped which raised concerns for agricultural workers' welfare. This opportunity provided the FairTrade industry with new partners and alternative products and sources of revenue.

The first products to become successful were coffee and tea, followed by dried fruits. Companies such as Cafe Direct were established to serve this need - it has now become a global brand. This company's approach introduced sophisticated marketing to this mass audience, with their focus on quality and a premium product. This aligned with the wider Fair Trade International organisation's approach.

"Our work is driven by informed consumer choices, and the desire of business to meet the expectations of their customers. Both of which provide crucial support for wider campaigning to reform international trade rules and create a fairer economic system."

Fair Trade acknowledges the need for circularity in the production and distribution of goods. It considers the consequences of production, but could it extend beyond the moment of consumption? Maybe to different sectors? There are certainly social needs which arise as a result of new technology. For example, shipping electronics to poor countries to be dismantled raises social issues similar to those that Fair Trade has been battling for decades. Acknowledging this new approach could bring a fresh full consumer lifecycle approach to the Fair Trade movement and extend benevolence beyond the beginning.

Food miles

Food miles is a term used to measure the distance between food production and consumption. Its wider aim is to highlight the environmental impact of some foods in transportation. Particular attention has been drawn to the air freighting of food from distant countries. The term was created by Tim Lang, Professor of Food Policy at the City University, London, who said: "The point was to highlight the hidden ecological, social and economic consequences of food production to consumers in a simple way, one which had objective reality but also connotations."[6]

Food Miles does well in simplifying the message. In most scenarios the measurement looks only at long haul from producers to store and point of purchase. The theme of miles travelled is a useful visualiser and one we will return to later in this chapter.

Carbon neutrality

Carbon neutrality has been a useful measure which captures the issue of greenhouse gas emissions and climate change through a simple equation. Businesses have started to communicate this to consumers. Doing this can help to build a mutual bond between consumer and company without requiring either party to stop the act of consumption. When revealed, it can be associated with the carbon effort of producing a product, or the wider impact of a company's operations.

Logitech have recently started to print the carbon impact of a product on their packaging. Initially, this is just for their gaming products, but it is planned to expand this to all their products by 2025. Bracken Darrell, CEO of Logitech, said in a recent Fast Company article *"We believe the best way to get companies to drop their carbon consumption is to make it a competitive marketplace around transparency, where consumers can see how much carbon is going into the things they buy".*[7] This is great for new purchases but doesn't provide details about the end of the product's life. Which is not so easy.

Tetrapak, who produce 190 billion packages every year, pride themselves on their environmental approach.[8] But they do admit the limitations of measuring the end of the product's life. *"The end-of-life treatment varies from case to case depending on local recycling conditions as well as the choices made by the end consumer. To calculate the exact footprint of each of these combinations would be a very lengthy task."*[9] So Tetrapak based their assumptions on European waste management averages - 47% recycling and 29% energy recovery, and landfill for the remaining 24%.[10]

The complexity of measuring these issues at on-boarding is huge - resources, logistics, haulage, assembly and distribution all need to be included. Hundreds of different suppliers are involved before the point of purchase. For each of these parties to measure an element such as carbon is no small task. But it has been achieved, and with increasing accuracy and compliance. Now the consumer understands carbon neutral approaches and can feel confident in supporting them at the on-boarding stage.

At off-boarding it is a different matter. Although there are far fewer operators involved in the process, the waste stream is enormously chaotic. The methods used at disposal are crude, ad-hoc and unmeasured. Laws and practices around disposal are still dictated locally. Until more effort is made to provide information about this part of the consumer lifecycle, it is going to be hard to see real transparency for the entire consumer lifecycle. The beginning is a known quantity, already under control and being assessed. The end is unknown, unconsidered and generally unguessable.

Energy at the end

The energy industry has had a relatively easy time communicating the environmental benefits of their product. It is now common for power companies to talk to their customers about solar, wind, biomass and hydro power. According to a report by The International Energy Agency (IEA), *"Renewable energy sources make up 26% of the world's electricity"*. The IEA expects capacity to expand 50% between 2019 and 2024, driven by solar, wind and hydropower projects.[11] These are sourcing issues sold at on-boarding to the consumer. Such issues are easy to package as pieces of marketing and are what a thoughtful consumer wants to align with today.

Many of the best energy companies also try to help consumers beyond the on-boarding of the product. They provide plenty of information about using energy economically and bring focus to the end of that experience through cost savings.

Using different payment types can open up different possibilities for saving money on energy consumption. Instead of just paying for its arrival at the consumer's home, new approaches could see the consumer being rewarded for keeping warmth in the home. This moves the perspective from on-boarding issues - such as creation, pricing and package - to off-boarding issues - storage, insulation and reduced emissions, for example. Such a shift in emphasis has a far greater impact on climate change and the environment.

Product disassembly

Designing for disassembly can be very beneficial for the end of a product's life. One of the early pioneers of Designing for Disassembly was Dr Joseph Chiodo, who worked on early investigations around design-related recycling solutions in the 1980's.[12] This was followed by his thesis in 1991 Design for Disassembly, which investigated automated approaches for what was considered a cumbersome process. Over the following decades he invented hundreds of approaches to, and mechanisms for disassembly. His work is now far more mainstream, especially in the circular economy and its supporters. The Cradle to Cradle Product Innovation Institute considers it an important part of a circular economy. This Institute was founded by the authors of the book Cradle to Cradle in 2010, William McDonough and Dr.Michael Braungart.

These are the six key Built Positive concepts endorsed by the Cradle to Cradle Product Innovation Institute:

- Circular Design
- Material Health
- Design for Disassembly, Reuse, and Recovery
- Value Chain Collaboration & Integration
- Realising Value
- Policies and Standards[13]

Design for Disassembly, Reuse, and Recovery encourages designers to create products and buildings "...*that can be easily deconstructed so that materials, products and components can be easily recovered, their value retained, to be meaningfully cycled.*"[14]

For the most part applications for disassembly have been limited to manufacturing. One of Dr Chiodo's innovations, for example, was a screw that would lose its thread when heated - making disassembly easier. This is, however, a technique that can really only be applied as part of a large manufacturing process. Additional obstacles to the widespread uptake of designing for disassembly have been market forces that pushed for cheaper and smaller products - this has been a common trend across consumerism and globalisation. A lack of consideration towards consumers is often a weakness of circular economy thinking. This tends to be dominated by manufacturing and material approaches, overlooking the powerful consumer drivers in the wider society.

Robots crushing it

Some companies are doing well in removing vulnerable human-beings from the dismantling process at the end of product life. Apple employ hundreds of robots to dismantle their reclaimed phones. This is an approach that came from a research and development project in 2016 called Liam.[15] The current, expanded iteration estimates that each robot will take apart 1.2 million devices a year. In 2018 Apple refurbished 7.8 million devices. This diverted 48,000 tons of e-waste from landfill. They are now recycling much of that reclaimed material in manufacturing - 100 percent of their own recycled tin goes into their logic boards, 100 percent recycled aluminium alloy goes into their MacBook Air and MacBook Mini products.[16]

This information about the Apple robots has been framed as a technical achievement, celebrated like a science fiction wonder: - "*Look! It's a robot*". But this negates the opportunity to see the issue as a social benefit - for example as saving low paid workers from risking serious health effects dismantling electronic products. Or putting pressure on competitor businesses to improve their reclaim and capture rates. This would also utilise the aftermath of the consumer experience as a place to consider social concerns.

E-Waste off-boarding choices

India has been burdened with e-waste. The dismantling of products containing hazardous materials in unsafe environments has become an enormous concern. Seelampur in Delhi is the largest e-waste dismantling area in India and one of the largest in the world. Children and adults work for 8 to 10 hours a day dismantling components. They are extracting precious metals like gold and copper, and pulling out functional components for resale. The processes used to do this work such as open incineration and acid-leeching, are often highly toxic.

According to TERI, The Energy and Resources Institute of India, *"There was 50 million tonnes of e-waste generated globally in 2018. Despite 66 per cent of the world's population being covered by e-waste legislation called the Basel Convention, only 20 per cent of global e-waste is recycled each year. Which means that 40 million tonnes of e-waste are either burned for resource recovery or illegally traded and treated in a sub-standard way."*[17]

The world is slowly becoming more aware of the end life of electronics as a dangerous part of the product lifecycle. Initiatives are being established, even in some of the biggest problem areas. Silicon Valley Toxics Coalition (SVTC) conducts research, pushes advocacy and grassroots organising *"...to promote human health and environmental justice in response to the rapid growth of the high-tech industry."*[18]

Electronics TakeBack Coalition[19] promotes green design and responsible recycling in the electronics industry. They focus on the health and wellbeing of workers and users, across the full lifecycle of the product. Much of the work taking place is generated by public policy and enforceable agreements. But more needs to be done around the consumer experience of the end life of the product. The problem needs to be dealt with before it leaves the customer, stopping it ending up in India being dismantled by a child.

Fairphone, the ethical phone manufacturer, offers an alternative to the campaign and pressure group approach. As they point out, their message comes from the source of consumption. *"From the earth to your pocket, a smartphone's journey is filled with unfair practices. We believe a fairer electronics industry is possible. By making change from the inside, we're giving a voice to people who care."*[20] They were also the first to integrate Fairtrade gold into their supply chain.[21] But the real key to their offering is the difference at the end of the consumer experience. Where many tech companies don't want the consumer to extend the battery life or update the camera themselves, Fairphone invites the consumer to do just that, thus extending the life of the product and having control at the end.

Waste miles

Waste miles is the distance waste has to go before being processed. This is a growing issue because of increased legislation around waste management. Products like oil, paint, batteries and mattresses, for example, require special processing that is not available at every waste processing location. As a result, much of it is hauled long distances from collection to a waste processing centre. According to the EEB Guide, an EU-funded Operational Lifecycle assessment study: *"Transport distances for different waste types may vary according to the number of treatment sites. For example, hazardous waste may have the longest transport distance, owing to the limited number of sites, whereas inert waste may have the shortest."*[22]

Even for recycled products, which many consumers would imagine are the most common elements in their waste, distance may well be greater than expected. Vivienne Walt a journalist for Fortune magazine highlighted the enormous changes in waste miles for recycled plastic in a 2020 article. While looking around a factory in Malaysia for her research, she saw the bales of plastic wrappers with familiar brands from her native United States. Some of the wrappers had travelled to be processed from Half Moon Bay, California, El Paso and Santa Monica. That is nearly 8000 miles. She went on to describe some of the background economics to the issue. *"The tidal wave of plastic items that enters the recycling stream each year is increasingly likely to fall right back out again, casualties of a broken market. Many products that consumers believe, and industries claim are "recyclable" are in reality not, because of stark economics. With oil prices near 20-year lows, so-called virgin plastic, a product of petroleum feedstocks, is now far cheaper and easier to obtain than recycled material."*[23]

In the last few years plastic recycling has been moving around the globe chasing cheaper labour and real estate prices. As the processing moves downstream, so does the safety. Workers are paid less, and ethics can become a distant concern. All the time the waste miles increase.

The difference between the beginning and the end can be stark. A benevolent consumer might buy an organic food product that is Fair Trade and after consumption separate the wrappings from that product carefully into recycling. The waste then travels out of the consumer's environment, across thousands of miles of sea, to unsafe workplaces and vulnerable people to process. This undoes all the good work they had understood they were doing at on-boarding.

Sanitation

According to the Gates Foundation *"More than half of the world's population, 4.5 billion people, continue to live without access to safely managed sanitation. In many cities in the global south, more than 50 percent of human waste escapes into the environment untreated."*[24]

This approach to sanitation hasn't really changed in hundreds of years. While in developed countries there is a network of thousands of pipes, from toilets to processing plants, using millions of gallons of water and enormous quantities of energy, millions of people in developing countries consume infected water due to sanitation problems.

In response, the Gates Foundation has established an initiative to develop a new type of toilet. This is one that requires minimum water and energy and avoids the requirement for networks of expensive pipes to support it.

The Reinvent the Toilet Challenge aims to create a toilet that:

- Removes germs from human waste and recovers valuable resources such as energy, clean water and nutrients.
- Operates "off the grid" without connections to water, sewer, or electrical lines.
- Costs less than US$.05 cents per user per day.
- Promotes sustainable and financially profitable sanitation services and businesses that operate in poor, urban settings.
- Is a truly aspirational next-generation product that everyone will want to use—in developed as well as developing nations.[25]

The Netflix documentary Inside Bill's Brain, covered some of this work. Dr. Sue Desmond-Hellmann, CEO of the Gates Foundation described the contrast between beginnings and ends, even in the philanthropic causes of global health. *"There is a global development area called WASH. It stands for Water, Sanitation and Hygiene. Most philanthropies work on clean water. Very few work on sanitation - which is toilet and sewage. There is nearly a complete lack of innovation on sanitation."*

Later in the show, Bill Gates talks about the illogical approach of just dealing with one end of the WASH issue. *"We can give people clean water. But if the kids are playing in mud which has human sewage in it, that is where all the diarrhoea infections are taking place."*[26]

Carbon impact credit card

Traditional, credit cards have put very little emphasis on carbon. In fact, any reflection about spending has been a distant thought to the design of credit products. Usually, the primary intention is to persuade the consumer to forget responsibility, encouraging the debt war-cry of 'Buy now, Pay later'. This could of course be applied equally to our responsibility for carbon impact.

After purchase and the thrill of shopping has faded, the consumer might be inspired to reflect about finances on reading their monthly statement. They are, however, unlikely to reflect on their carbon impact, which often remains invisible to the consumer throughout the consumer lifecycle. This, thankfully, is starting to change with the help of better tools for gauging carbon impact, new approaches to financial products and consumers who want more integrity in consumption.

A leader in this area is Ålands Index Solutions.[27] This is a Swedish start-up, first created in 2015 by Ålandsbanken. Their intention was to inform consumers about the impact of their purchases on the planet. By using an extensive database of products and the carbon required to create them, Ålands Index can estimate the impact of a person's purchases. Their success has attracted some world class collaborators, such as Standard & Poors Global Ratings, and MasterCard. It is now integrated into many established banking products through an easy-to-use API. Ålands Index Solutions has also created a consumer side of the business called Doconomy[28] — we will talk to the founders later in the book. They are shortly releasing two credit cards that present the company's vision directly to consumers.

As a consumer experience, this brings the carbon impact of a person's purchase sharply into focus at on-boarding. It presents it to the consumer as empowering and actionable. It does away with the powerless shaming that the consumer usually experiences with such engagements. The language and positioning of the Ålandsbanken product plays with the traditional credit card message. Their standard offering, The White Card, helps the consumer *"Track, measure and compensate for your carbon footprint every day."* The Black Card, comes *"With no premium benefits except for the world's first built-in CO_2 emissions limit, creating the very foundation for conscious consumption."*

It is refreshing and inspiring to see this type of product, which mixes the beginning and the end of the consumer experience. It works against the irresponsible short-term debt purchase so common with credit cards and stresses the long-term concerns for climate change and carbon.

Benevolent opportunities at the end

The opportunities for benevolent consumer experiences at off-boarding are numerous, diverse and complicated, but not impossible. In summarising the broad issues of benevolent consumer experiences at on-boarding and off-boarding, we can make some assumptions about the characteristics of both.

Many of the problems considered have emerged as a result of mass consumerism. Although the solutions proposed aim to improve those issues, they are still being promulgated via a commercial system. Even when one needy cause is sorted, another consequential one may happen after consumption.

The on-boarding experience incorporates a significant quantity of persuasion tools with branding and marketing. These locate the benevolent cause in the context of a consumer experience. The consumer experience has been developed over decades - we can see this as a. It has established behaviours that limit interest and responsibility past product usage and rarely live onto the off- boarding experience.

We can define these in to two areas, one is an ascending trajectory towards the consumer. This is well organised and persuasive. The other is a descending trajectory away from the consumer. Which is chaotic, overlooked and emotionally repulsive.

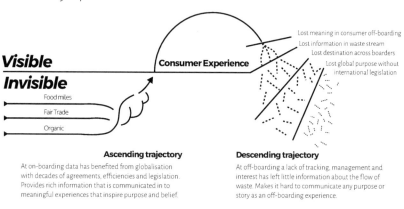

Ascending trajectory

At on-boarding data has benefited from globalisation with decades of agreements, efficiencies and legislation. Provides rich information that is communicated in to meaningful experiences that inspire purpose and belief.

Descending trajectory

At off-boarding a lack of tracking, management and interest has left little information about the flow of waste. Makes it hard to communicate any purpose or story as an off-boarding experience.

Data is one key to improvement. After decades of trade, tax and logistical alignment between nations, there is now detailed knowledge about the flow of goods between producer and consumer. Representing this to the consumer as a story can be inspiring when framing a benevolent issue. The off-boarding and aftermath of products and waste is far less well documented. Much of this data is based on assumptions and manual field research. This is harder to quantify, capture and communicate meaningfully. But there are opportunities. Some I have captured below.

Data improvement

The work we considered by Ålandsbanken and their Ålands Index helps build data and knowledge, not only for the consumer, but also for business or charities to reveal more detailed benevolent causes. Likewise, the increase in technology at the source of some of these issues - for example the toilet systems that the Gates Foundation is working on - could also help capture more data about usage and need. This would build a richer story around this cause.

Extended concerns

Dirty plastics and broken toilets are not very attractive to the benevolent consumer. Communicating charitable needs around such issues is a significant challenge. Much of this type of charity work requires donations and is hard to link to a consumer product purchase. A potential resolution would see similar causes extending their coverage. Fair Trade electronics dismantling would benefit from this.

New routes

A key change would be to avoid the normal route of departure. There was a time when there were only regular mass-produced oranges. Social concern saw problems and defined an *"alternative"* with an Organic Orange. Different routes to market had to be created to increase this diversity of choice. Likewise, new routes for departure will be required to bring new opportunities to endings.

Can we imagine independent waste processing companies presenting themselves as an ethical solution? For a small fee they could dismantle and process e-waste locally. This would neutralise the assets fully and provide clear evidence and documented authenticity.

Direct liability instead of labels

Consumers may become more detail-oriented in the future. They might require direct evidence beyond a company simply being a member of an ethical organisation and placing a label on a product. Failings have been seen in the palm oil industry and the Roundtable on Sustainable Palm Oil - RSPO. According to a Greenpeace investigation, two-thirds of the 30 members were involved in the Indonesian forest fires in 2019. The report also linked members of RSPO to a further 1.2 million hectares of fires across Indonesia since 2015.

Head of Forests at Greenpeace UK, Richard George said *"Consumers are being conned by 'certified sustainable palm oil'. A phrase that's bandied about by supermarkets and big brands attempting to distance themselves from deforestation."*[29]

Tethering of materials to manufacturer and individual

Consumers are proud to display their benevolent consumption. Sharing it on social media is common. This bonding between provider and producer needs to be extended to off-boarding. Product numbers, production dates and other identifiers help to connect manufacturer and consumer elsewhere across the consumer lifecycle. More needs to be done to connect them long term. For example, supplying envelopes to return dismantled parts could be an issue business begins to have pride in.

Companies who offer involvement across the whole consumer lifecycle would have closer bonds with the consumer. Providing ethical choices at on-boarding can continue though the consumer lifecycle to off-boarding.

Full life impact

It is a welcome step to see more companies revealing the carbon impact of the products they create. This is only half the story. Assessing accurately how that product completes its lifecycle will be a critical next step. Integration of Scope 3 Greenhouse Gas emissions requires end of life assessments. Manufacturers will need to know better about their product at the end of its life and not rely on assumptions and averages.

Doconomy: Carbon impact credit card

In August 2020 I spoke with the founders of Doconomy, Mathias Wikstrom and Johan Pihl, to ask them more about the Doconomy product (doconomy.com).

They first met at Cannes Lions after both winning awards: Mathias for the Baltic Sea Project and Johan for the the Humanium Metal Initiative. So, they come with heaps of experience with social change and environmental issues, but also with a strong understanding of the consumer and marketing. This gives them a unique mix of skills in developing innovative new products for a sustainable future. The Doconomy credit card product is their latest.

Joe: *I wanted to start by asking a bit about the background of the product and how did it get started?*

Johan: *Going back to the very beginning, it was related to a project we created with Ålandsbanken. That ended up being the Ålands Index. Which was the first time carbon impact was measured per transaction.*

Joe: *Was that the first time globally any company had done it?*

Johan: *Yes. And that was back in 2014. Now Ålandsbanken is one of the founding partners of Doconomy. So, there is a strong connection there. We basically looked for a new way to explore the potential of how the consumer understands their carbon footprint. That is the starting point.*

Joe: *Why did you pick the credit card? I have always considered it as the worst example of guilt free, reckless consumption.*

Mathias: *If we were to select a specific point in time to illustrate consumption then it is the transaction. Because the transaction moment is an action in trust. It is an exchange. We are trying to inject responsibility at the very core of that moment. That is why the credit card as a vehicle for increased responsibility and transparency is so important. The credit card could be the guilty tool of mass destruction as it can aid mass consumption. In many ways, what we are doing with Doconomy, is highjacking current systems and functions and rewiring them to become more sustainable.*

Joe: *It strikes me as a very reflective tool. Which isn't what credit cards are about.*

Johan: *If you would get a load of people to re-design the credit card. Most would approach faster, cheaper, etc. And this is what you see with many of the new fin-tech banks starting up. They want to speed up consumption. We have decided to go in the other direction, that the consumer should be more reflective. Take more time to consider the monthly bill, what is the real impact.*

Joe: *Your business seems to understand that it must be part of the consumer experience.*

Johan: *Yes. A sustainable lifestyle. We are not interested in politics. We are creating a tool, with a built-in responsibility to indicate your consumption to the planet. It is deliberately staying away from any judgement or guilt.*

Mathias: *At the end of the day this is an educational effort. We aim to help consumers understand. Our perspective is a friendly one.*

We know the world is in a place where we don't want to be. How the hell can we get out of it? Transparency is one of the greatest tools.

Joe: *I find it so hard to off-set carbon with current systems and apps. The amount of detail I need to add, it seems like doing a science project.*

Johan: *I love this problem. Our ability to develop a new, consumer-centric way of doing off-setting is obviously part of our plan at Doconomy. It is so important to get right. If you look at all the banking products that are long term. For example, pensions and investments. You have to ask, why isn't off-setting part of that? That is why it is one of the critical areas that we are looking into. We really need to get off-setting right.*

Joe: *When I do presentations about endings at businesses, I am often surprised by the lack of acknowledgement of a product ending. Which I see as a blindness to the consequences of product creation.*

Johan: *Right now, we are still in an era of redundantness. We will soon see an era of companies that are sustainable by nature. We have not seen completely how they will create their products yet. We still see people and businesses that are tangled up in emotion.*

Mathias: *It is like pretending the problem doesn't go away. But I think as long as the job is getting done. It is hard to tell who is green-washing. Everyone has a different starting point. For example, I would find it hard working with oil companies. But actually, that is maybe the best place to start.*

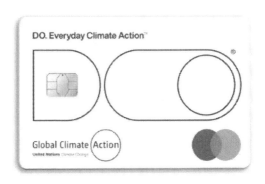

Doconomy credit card.

Electrolux: Recycled vacuum cleaner

An investigation by four Swedish companies exposed fascinating insights about product end of life and consumer off-boarding. Stena Recycling, a waste management company, ABB, a robot manufacturing company, Combitech, an analytics company and Electrolux, a home appliance manufacturer, worked with each other's strengths to pull together on a waste processing issue for the future. The aim was to find improvements in circularity in the waste stream. They found that they could identify, remove and dissemble a product from regular e-waste as it goes through processing.

An article from Combitech describes the process "*The waste is scanned to identify product and material with data from the manufacturer, the robot determines which parts can be recycled*

and carries out the disassembly. The result is less losses and better quality of what is recycled. Which contributes to more sustainable production and consumption."[1]

After the initial successful investigation, Stena and Electrolux took the project further with one particular product - a vacuum cleaner.[2] The project revealed how each company's role will evolve in a future where society needs to achieve circularity on thousands of products.

Amanda Molina Zoppas, Sustainability Lead for Wellbeing at Electrolux and one of the key people in the circular vacuum cleaner project, kindly agreed to talk at an Endineering course I ran in Stockholm in 2021. She told the students and me about the project and the insights they had gained. The project succeeded in producing a vacuum cleaner made of

100% recycled materials and reused components. It was sourced from a wide range of discarded products, including hair dryers, computers and other vacuum cleaners. A prototype for change, the project aimed at creating an example of a more sustainable product through circular thinking, as well as establishing new types of cross-industry collaboration within the circular economy context.

As part of the project, the team also investigated the state of the vacuum cleaners found in the flow of Waste Electric and Electronic Equipment (WEEE) that Stena collected. Surprisingly, many components were still functional. And even more surprising was discovering that motors still had on average 83% lifetime left. This meant that most people had disposed of their product before the end of its capability.

These insights helped Amanda and the team build a range of new offerings that aimed to help people keep their current products for longer. For example, making it easier to buy a single replacement part for a product might stop people believing that the whole product needs to be thrown away.

It is inspiring to hear about the bonding of these businesses which proves that practical circularity with end of life products can be achieved. It is also important to hear how much can be discovered when we study the end of consumer lifecycle and how much we can improve consumerism with that knowledge.

The second iteration of this project was revealed at the Circular Initiative conference in July 2021: Electrolux and Stena Recycling have developed the 2-Infinity prototype vacuum cleaner. This aims to deliver a 90% recyclable product.[1]

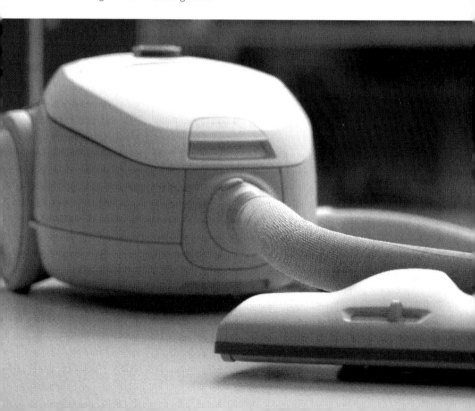

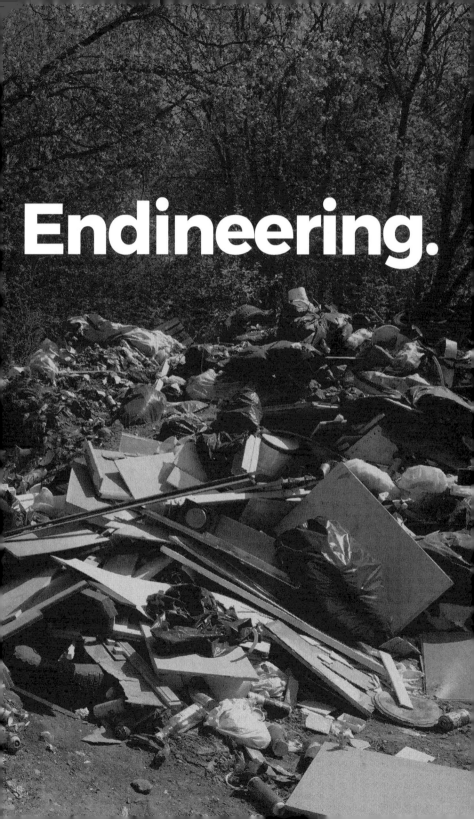

Ch.9

What is 'endineering'?

'Endineering' is a shorthand term which refers to the practice, philosophy, tools and methods of creating consumer off-boarding experiences of a product, service or digital product. This is as opposed to on-boarding, which relates to the beginning of the product experience and involves a wealth of established industries who supply meaning, instruction and encouragement to transport the consumer from passive observer to engaged customer. The off-boarding experience takes an engaged and active customer through the final stages of ownership or usage to a meaningful ending of the product relationship – *an engineered ending*.

'Endineering' aims to increase understanding of the off-boarding experience in the consumer lifecycle, inspiring specific elements which can be incorporated into product experiences. These elements combine to mitigate problems which may occur in the last phase of consumerism. They aim to guide the consumer through the final stages of their engagement to achieve a better and less damaging ending. These improvements can be broad-reaching across environmental, humanitarian, technological, social or emotional areas.

'Endineering' can be applied across many factors. At a high level it draws comparisons across sectors to reveal common societal problems in consumerism. From these insights I propose principles, processes and tools thoughout this book. These can then be applied more specifically across industry sectors and inspire product development, creating tangible touchpoints throughout the customer journey. The type of transaction model a business uses at on-boarding influences their ability to engage meaningfully at off-boarding. An example is a packaging solution that empowers a consumer to return items once concluded. A further example could be a method of sharing a photo that helps the un-sharing of it later.

'Endineering' aims to improve consumerism. Although it is not anti-business, it recognises clearly that our current pace, approach and philosophy around consumerism cannot continue. It also sees failures in our current approach to sustainability, which so often seems to be created without the consumer experience being a considered aspect.

'Endineering' aims to change many of the outdated and damaging practices in consumerism by inspiring a new way to look for solutions to some of consumerism's most challenging problems.

Ch.10

The aim at the end.

A good consumer off-boarding experience should be...connected consciously to the rest of the experience through **emotional triggers** that are **measurable and actionable** by the user.
It should **identify and bond the consumer and provider together in mutual responsibility.** It's aim should be to **neutralise the negative consequences of consumption.** It should be **concluded in a timely manner and avoid assets falling outside the consumer lifecycle.**

Let's look at the implications of these suggestions in greater detail.

Consciously connected

The consumer experience should feel similar at both the beginning and the end of the consumer lifecycle. The experience should feel branded in the same way. The same narrative voice should off-board the consumer from the experience, with similar principles and tone of voice as when they were being on-boarded.

Currently, many off-boarding experiences are delivered without care or interest from the provider. Further still, off-boarding is sometimes delivered by entirely different groups – municipal organisations such as waste management, or health and safety representatives for example. The consumer should be under no illusion that off-boarding and on-boarding are from the same body.

Emotional triggers

The emotional richness delivered at on-boarding helps consumers to engage. These feelings should be matched at off-boarding, inspiring engagement and interest from all parties. Emotional triggers should offer an opportunity for the consumer to reflect personally on the experience gained. This should also benefit the provider, promoting the brand and carrying a passionate message beyond the usage period. The provider should also be demonstrating their credentials in issues around consumerism at this point. Being present as a brand both emotionally and actively is important at the end. Currently many brands seem to struggle with appearing authentic. Accusations of greenwashing or selling people's privacy reflect this poor level of emotional engagement at the end.

Measurable and actionable

Consumers should have a clear, measurable understanding of the impact of their consumption at off-boarding. This information should be couched in a way which enables the consumer to reflect upon their involvement in consumerism and be empowered to do something about it.

Businesses and governments around the world need to build and agree upon common measuring systems that are easily understandable by the consumer. There needs to be a culture of education and engagement in these new measuring values to fully support them. This would help to establish a language that helps the consumer and the provider to communicate and bond over the status of lingering assets, whether these be digital, service or physical product endings. Some of these endings might take decades to neutralise.

Identify and bond consumer and provider

The specific, individual identity of the consumer needs to be universally recognised and tethered to the provider.

An individual has many identities as a result of being a consumer – personal credit scores, loyalty cards, quantities of followers. These reflect a person's capacity to consume. In comparison, after consumption a person's identity is reduced to their being a passive witness – worrying about climate change or plastic in the sea.

Society needs to attach personal identity to consumerism. Consumers should be recognised as perpetrators of their past consumer activity. Currently, the physical fall out of consumption is too easily relinquished, shipped overseas or left in the atmosphere for the most vulnerable in the world and future generations to grapple with.

Further to this, the consumer can't be abandoned to deal with this responsibility alone. It has to be done in partnership with the provider, tied to the neutralising of assets. Businesses need to move beyond relationships limited to a 'good usage experience' and start to be proud partners with consumers working towards a healthier conclusion.

Neutralising the negative consequences of consumption

Consumers need to be offered clear routes to neutralising the assets of consumption. Currently, many of the routes towards off-boarding a consumer experience focus on speed. Here the consumer and provider can leave the crime scene very fast. This approach exploded in the last century with disposable products. But exactly the same culture has been adopted in services and digital relationships. For example, the carbon legacy of an aeroplane flight can last for decades, but both consumer and provider are absolved from this responsibility. Similarly, with digital – assets such as offensive comments and photos can easily be left lingering without consequences for years.

Neutralising the assets of consumption should be the joint responsibility of both consumer and provider. People understand how some products – vegetable matter for example are neutralised through organic decay. Other assets, like recycled plastics, appear to have smooth, accessible routes to off-boarding courtesy of municipal recycling bins and collections. But it's what happens afterwards that is less visible. Plastic often gets shipped to vulnerable countries where people who are unprotected by safety laws process the material. Although the plastic material might eventually be neutralised, the consequences have knock on effects.

Businesses, consumers and, arguably, wider society need to see the issue of neutralising assets as an integral consumerism experience. For example, one simple improvement would be changing what is communicated at the end of product life. Producers need to stop talking about material capability and start talking about neutralising routes, locations and schedules. For example, they should stop saying this is *"Recyclable"* - which is hard to define and start giving details such as *"This product is dismantled by x method and then gets recycled by x process, at this place in x country. This process is completed within this amount of time and costs this amount of carbon, which is then off-set."*

Of course, proper neutralising will not be as precise as this. It will require more details, explanation, education and clarity. But this is critical to moving consumerism to a better place.

Timely manner and avoiding assets falling outside the consumer lifecycle

Businesses need to intervene at the end of the lifecycle with an active and attentive attitude. If the consumer experience is left to linger on beyond a planned ending, the assets become outdated, obsolete and risk falling out of control into the wider environment. This has become normal in recent decades, thus promoting indifference about unused products, accounts and subscriptions.

Businesses will need to redefine timeframes and style of engagement with the consumer. In the short term, they will need to engage actively with the consumer in order to put an end to unused assets that linger in the physical, digital and service landscapes. This will seem counter-intuitive to a business culture that has, in the past, benefitted from overlooking endings. But, in the long term, businesses that get this right will benefit from deeper, more loyal partnerships based on trusted re-engagement over years. Strategic approaches will become more sophisticated, not only with regard to the consumer experience and long-term impact, but also as a means of collaboration to improve consumerism.

Ch.11

Ends at on-boarding.

Even before the consumer purchases something, aspects of the consumption experience will be framing the end of the process. Emotional messages that the consumer receives at the beginning will create emotional expectations at the end. Such messages will be characterised by how they are communicated, the personality of the consumer and the resolution of the whole process at off-boarding. The way in which financial arrangements have been made determine how the end is positioned. Physical assets provided at the beginning will enable or ruin environmental opportunities at off-boarding. The promises made about the duration of the product will define expectations about usage time and create a perceived off-boarding sequence. Legal rights impact on empowerment and frame the type of resolution at the end. Not only being aware of these issues, but actively engaging with them as a business will help to deliver the best ending for your customers.

In this section we will consider some of the elements relating to the beginning of the consumer experience that influence the end.

On-boarding

One of the most knowledgeable people in the business of on-boarding is Krystal Higgins. She is a veteran of the digital industry who has helped

Google, Ebay and Nvidia with their on-boarding and user experience issues. She is also author of the book Better Onboarding. Krystal and I spoke at a conference in 2020 and found lots of common ground between on-boarding and off-boarding, particularly how important each area is to the other. She puts it like this.

"One thing that really helps on-boarding shine is a thoughtful approach to the off-boarding, or ending, experience. This is very important when considering an onboarding experience which is meant to encourage new users to sign up for, subscribe to, or buy something. It requires trust. Trust can be built by removing the risk of someone making the choice to commit. This can be partly achieved by offering new users an ability to try out core parts of your product before they make a commitment, but also by illustrating how they can reverse their decision later by reassuring them that it will be easy to delete an account, cancel a subscription, or return something they bought. Having a solid off-boarding strategy."[1]

In the following passages we will consider aspects of on-boarding that indicate and influence the experience of the end.

Product duration

When a physical product is bought, messages about how long the product might be expected to last are drowned out in the noise of the product's usage benefits. This is problematic when the environmental impact of physical products is higher than for most areas of consumerism. Plastics are a clear example of this. Increasing awareness in the consumer of how long a product might last would greatly increase engagement at the end and benefit society's abilities to recapture products at end of life. It would also increase the opportunity for businesses to engage with the consumer, collaborate around disposability and - potentially - create fertile ground for the next sales cycle.

Sell-by and use-by dates

In most countries' food companies are legally expected to state how long a product will be consumable. Some countries, the U.S. for example, believe it should be at the discretion of the manufacturer to put this on products. *"FDA does not require food firms to place "expired by", "use by" or "best before" dates on food products."*[2]

The UK requires a *"best-before"* date, which focuses on quality. The food will be safe to eat after this date but may not be at its best. Its flavour and texture might not be as good. Use-by dates focus on safety. Foods can be eaten until the *"use by"* date, after which they may cause harm.[3]

Cosmetic endings

In the cosmetics and toiletries industry there are indicators to tell the consumer how long an item can be open for before its best time has passed. There are two types:

The 'Best Before End Of...' which often uses the egg cup graphic and then a date.

The 'Period After Opening...' symbol which indicates how long a product will be usable after opening. This is usually indicated in months, inside a graphic of an open jar. [4]

Best Before End Of

Period After Opening

Best Before End Of Period After Opening

The majority of product duration information labels are provided for safety reasons. They are presented in simple numbers, taking up as little space on the packaging as possible. In many cases this comes across as passive information which is not directly actionable. It normally lacks further off-boarding instructions - an example would be: '*Wash, break apart, recycle as plastic*'.

Might product end dates be applied to other product types? Imagine if consumers were told how long the average phone lasts? Or for how many years a cheap piece of furniture might be safe to use? Some would argue that the product's warranty fulfils this need. But I think that while it suggests the physical capability of the product, it doesn't indicate the average usage period. For example, a phone could work for a decade on a functional level, but on average the majority get used for 24 months. Changing this might seem a subtle detail, but in terms of consumer experience it could be significant. Including a potential usage period might raise significant questions about consumption and inspire the consumer to think beyond the purchase and usage stages of the consumer lifecycle and consider long term responsibilities. One of those responsibilities might be mending a device.

Repairability score

The consumer can now see how hard it might be to mend something before they have even bought it. As part of a wide-ranging Right to Repair initiative being taken across Europe, France has made it mandatory to show the repairability of electrical products up front. The Repairability Index scores a product between 0 – not repairable – 10 easily repairable.[5]

This needs to be displayed at point of sale of the product, whether in store or online. Below is an example of the Repairability Index score of a Samsung Galaxy Z Flip on the French Amazon store.

Passez la souris sur l'image pour zoomer

Samsung Galaxy Z Flip3 5G - 256Go - Smartphone Android débloqué - Version Française - Noir

Visiter la boutique Samsung

Prix : 1 109,00 €
Tous les prix incluent la TVA.

Précommande garantie au plus bas prix ! Détails ˅

DigitalStorageCapacity: **Veuillez sélectionner**

128 Go

Couleur: **Veuillez sélectionner**

Digital duration dates

At the beginning of many of our online experiences, we are often asked to accept 'Cookies'. Cookies are a small bit of code that help the website remember who the person is. A shopping basket is a good example of this, when a person adds something, then leaves the site. On their return the site knows it is them because the cookie recognises their computer.

On arrival at a new website the individual is presented with a consent form that tells them about the cookies - who owns them, what they do and their expiry date. The person should be able to see this clearly and even select preferences as to which cookies they will consent to. But how long should that consent last? The ePrivacy Directive, which is the practical end of the EU's GDPR law,[6] say they should not last longer than 12 months, but in practice, they could remain on your device much longer if you do not take action to remove them.

There are two basic types of cookie:

Session cookies – these cookies are temporary and expire once you close your browser (or once your session ends).

Persistent cookies — all persistent cookies have an expiration date written into their code, but their duration can vary.[7] For example after 1 day, 1 week, 1 year, etc.

Let's look at an example from an average consumer electronics website - Digital Trends.[8] Digging around on this website before I consent to cookies, I can look through the details of each cookie. It is very revealing. The chart below examples only a few of the hundreds of cookies being used on that website. What it shows more than anything is how little consideration there is about the end of the lifespan of the cookie.

Who	Status / Reason	Expiry	In years
Amazon	Pending	5758 days	15 years
Google	Pending	6489 days	17 years
Hulu.com	Pending	3652 days	10 years
Acuity	Pending	24837 days	68 years
adt.com	Pending	36525	100 years
homedepot.com	Pending	599999 days	1642 years
Digital Trends	Pending	2914550 days	7979 years

Let's put some of these numbers in to a human perspective. I am in my late 40's. Even with my best intentions I am not going to live much longer than 90 years. So, Acuity's consent is going to be worthless, because I would probably have been dead for a decade or so before it expires. Likewise, adt. com's request for consent at 100 years is surely pointless. Then we get into the world of ludicrous consent lifespan. Home Depot is asking for me to approve something for 599999 days. Which is 1642 years. That is a big ask. I am certainly dead, as are, multiple generations of my ancestors. On the upside it assumes that we survived climate change. Yay!

If we reversed the direction of that approval. It would go back to 378 AD, which is near the end of the Roman Empire, just before the sacking of Rome in 410 AD.[9] Imagine the forethought of a Roman citizen approving something that would expire in this year. Imagine their lack of knowledge of what was coming over the following 1600 years - the printing press, penicillin, human flight, electricity, and the internet.

But if that doesn't stun your mind regarding absent endings in your cookie consent, then maybe the Digital Trends website's own cookie will make your mind melt. It is 2914550 days. Which is 7979 years.

If we went a similar distance back in time it would take us to 6000 BC - the time of Paleolithic hunter- gatherer communities, long before the bronze age at 3000BC.[10] Imagine a person of that time, equipped with little more than a spear or flint, trying to grapple with the forethought needed to approve consent until the year 2020.

I think we seriously need some sober thinking in cookie end dates.

Terms and conditions

The terms and conditions at the beginning of the consumer experience establish the boundaries of many consumer relationships. However, most consumers overlook the small print in a rush to make the purchase. ProPrivacy, a digital privacy advocate group, ran a survey asking people to sign up for terms and conditions. In them they hid ludicrous requests such as - give your mom permission to review your internet browsing history - and another that handed over naming rights to your firstborn child.[11]

They also found that respondents lied about reading the agreement - 70% claimed they had read the agreement, 33% claiming they had read the agreement in detail. Amazingly, ProPrivacey found only 1% of people read the terms and conditions agreement. This reveals how little consumers really engage with what can be significant consequences and how unsuccessful

terms and conditions are as a method of engagement.

Consumers could be forgiven for not being engaged in terms and conditions, given the language used. Phrases and wording that anyone would find disturbing are often included. As part of the research for the first Ends book, I read (yes, really) the Apple iTunes Terms amounting to more than 20,000 words. There were many disturbing phrases. For example, *"Apple reserves the right to disband a Family in accordance with the "Termination" section of this Agreement."* This I thought was so funny, I put it on a t-shirt and got my kids to wear it. Which produced some strange looks from people as they walked past.

Forced arbitration

Forced arbitration is a common clause buried deep in the terms and conditions which protects businesses and exposes consumers. Few consumers have any idea what it is or that they have agreed to it. It is easily missed at the beginning of the consumer experience, yet removes consumer rights at the end.

In boring legal terms, according to the American Arbitration Association it says this...

"Any controversy or claim arising out of or relating to this contract, or the breach thereof, shall be settled by arbitration administered by the American Arbitration Association in accordance with its Commercial [or other] Arbitration Rules, and judgment on the award rendered by the arbitrator(s) may be entered in any court having jurisdiction thereof."[12]

What it means in everyday terms is if a consumer has a problem with a product – it breaks, hurts them, kills them or anything in between - they have to take that issue up outside the court system and resolve it directly with the producer. They are also not allowed to group together with other customers in a class action. So, they have to do it on their own. This puts the individual in a weakened position, as they have fewer resources than a big company. These clauses first emerged in telecoms and financial services, but have recently spread further across consumer sectors. It is common to use them in the US. According to a 2019 study in the UC Davis Law Review, 81 of the 100 largest U.S. companies now use arbitration in their dealings with consumers.[13] Fifteen of the largest 20 U.S. credit card issuers, and 7 of the 8 largest cell phone companies use arbitration. It is also used by Amazon.com.[14]

Returns policy

A common ending, which may be experienced early on in the consumer lifecycle, is returning goods. When a consumer rejects their product, some retailers have embraced this opportunity. They consider the returns process as an opportunity to show off their customer experience qualities. Making sure a consumer feels confident about the returns policy is key to making them feel comfortable with the initial purchase and trusting the brand. This increases the potential for a purchase later on.

The success of online sales, and the smoothness of return processes, is reflected in its growth over recent years, especially at Christmas. The courier service UPS estimated 1.9 million returns in the US on the first business day of January and expected a 26 percent increase from the previous year.[15] In the UK, the Royal Mail call the first Monday after Christmas 'Mail Back Monday', because of the large quantity of returns that people send.[16]

The best fashion businesses allow a customer to return an item within a year. If they can provide evidence of the sale with a receipt, then most offer a full refund. Some, for example Nordstrom, have no time limits on returns.[17]

Return policies abused

Some customers have been known to abuse the system of returns. They purchase an item, wear it only once and then return it and reclaim the money. It has even become part of popular culture to keep tags on clothing and wear them for a single occasion. Companies are starting to counter this trend. Macy's have started to place large clothing tags on their products which say *"Do not remove"* and refuse to exchange items that don't have the tag when returned. Target and Walmart refuse to exchange inflatable beds and any reading material.[18]

Some individuals return items so often they get noticed by companies. Research by Brightpearl, a resource planning company, found 45% of UK retailers, including brands Asos and Harrods, are considering blacklisting serial returners.

A recent article in the UK's Independent newspaper by Sabrina Barrasked, asked some serial returners for their reasoning. Sophie Cridland, a freelance journalist from Dorset in the UK said *"I have quite big feet, I'm a size eight and so sometimes I have to try out the shoes first to see whether they are too big or too small. If they do start clamping down and I get penalised, I won't be shopping with them anymore because it's not worth paying that postage every time"*. Another person described the benefits and thrills. Sarah from the West Midlands said *"I love the thrill of a shop and buying new clothes. Putting on something new makes me feel really happy and excited. I think that feeling has turned me into a returnaholic."* [19]

Financial systems are changing to adapt to this new consumer behaviour. For example, Klarna, a Swedish FinTech company, provides their customers with three payment methods to use on websites like Asos - Pay here and now, Get first. Pay Later, Pay a little now and then. [20] In their advertising Klarna makes a big deal of the freedom customers should feel when shopping. They support the short-term consumer lifecycle when a dress is returned after a single use.

Experiencing payment

Within marketing there are enormous fields of research looking at pricing and how best to motivate the consumer. Research by Prelec and Loewenstein (1998) proposed that consumers have a preference for paying after purchase when the purchase is a utilitarian type of product - for example a washing machine. They want to avoid or postpone the pain of payment. They are exhibiting an *"aversion to making a payment when the utility from consumption is forgone".* [21] In contrast, they found that people enjoyed prepaying for hedonic types of experiences, for example a holiday.

Further research by Okada (2005) defined hedonic purchases based on *"wants"*, and utilitarian purchases based on *"shoulds"*. The type of purchase a person looks forward to (wants) can be defined as "approach motivation". People make this type of purchase with pleasurable anticipation - a holiday. People make a utilitarian type of purchase with a focus on avoiding negative outcomes. This can be defined as *"avoidance motivation"*.

This research was built upon by Vanessa M. Patrick and Whan Park, [22] who considered the additional dimension of durable and non-durable purchases relating to the payment before or after question. They found that a hedonistic non-durable purchase produced the highest preference for prepayment.

Patrick and Park felt the Apple iMac 3g computers of circa 1998-2003, were good examples of a design that *"increases consumers' savouring and anticipation of consumption, leading them to be willing to prepay (even at a premium price) for an essentially functional purchase".*

Rapanui: Provider and consumer bond

Rapanui Clothing (www.rapanuiclothing.com) is a T Shirt company working with natural materials, renewable energy and plastic-free packaging. Returning the product at the end is considered central to their consumer experience.

Rapanui Clothing have thought about the end early on in their product development. The founders, Mart and Rob, have felt strongly, not just about the material side of the business, but the consumer side. They don't make excess products. Each order is fulfilled uniquely at time of order. They say *"Everything we make is designed from the start to be sent back when it is worn out."* 1

They show a clear route to enable the consumer to deliver the best end possible. *"It's free to send our products back to us, and we pay the postage in the UK. We'll recover and remanufacture the material into a new product, and we'll reward you with a* *coupon that you can use to save money on your next purchase."* 2

It is common for companies to talk about sustainability in their manufacturing nowadays. They offer their circular economy credentials and quote their use of recycled materials and sustainable sources. But few talk about the consumer's role in this. The circularity tends to begin with the resources and end once the product has been sold. This overlooks the consumer's critical role in the whole process. Without this, the process is far from being circular.

Rapanui make the consumer offboarding experience visible, actionable and creates a bond between the customer and themselves.

Returning the product at the end is considered central to their consumer experience.

Example.

Stuffstr: Re-circulating at the end

The company Stuffstr wants all products to be constantly moving through the consumer lifecycle. By doing this they have learnt a great deal about building an off-boarding experience and putting the end at the heart of their customer journey. In an interview for Insider Trends, co-founder and CEO John Atcheson talked about the vision of Stuffstr.

"We believe every item produced should be used fully, then reprocessed and used again."[1] This requires making off-boarding as seamless as on-boarding. Atcheson says *"The business was originally founded with the idea of fundamentally changing the flow of post-sale."*[2] They knew early on this can't be done from the sidelines, like a second hand shop operation. He reflected on the company's early proposition *"If we are ever going to do that at scale, then we have to be tied into the source and be partnered with those who actually sell these products."*[3]

This is a key step to keeping the consumer and the provider bonded and stopping the assets of consumption from falling outside the consumer lifecycle.

Stuffstr's success has come from making sure the end of the consumer journey is as easy as possible. In Atcheson's words *"You don't need to simply reduce the friction in the process; you need to eliminate it. You need to make it easy for people to be able to re-circulate things when they are done with them, rather than let them pile up in closets and attics and then gather everything together every year and go dump it somewhere. Otherwise, you're back to where people need to do something, such as taking pictures and entering information."*[4] Which becomes a burdensome off-boarding experience.

"If we are ever going to do that at scale, then we have to be tied into the source and be partnered with those who actually sell these products."

John Atcheson.
co-founder and CEO

How it works

- Stuffstr partners with a store that the consumer uses

- They collect up to 5 years' worth of purchase data

- Items purchased then appear on the App

- The customer can see the prices of currently owned clothes

- The customer accepts prices and gathers clothes

- Items get picked up free of charge

- Then the customer gets a voucher to use with the retailer they originally bought the item from.

- The customer returns to the store and buys a new item.

Five transaction types

Payment after delivery
When a consumer pays for a service after receiving it. Common in hairdressing, restaurants, taxis (at least the old sort), and a host of other consumer experiences.

Payment before delivery
When the consumer pays before receiving the service or the product. Common in transport, like flights and train travel, also in concerts and a variety of live entertainment experiences. But also, a large majority of product exchanges are paid for before receiving the delivery.

Scheduled payment
When the transaction happens on a scheduled basis, for example by direct debit through monthly payments via a bank. Common in subscription services and utility companies.

Synchronous payment
When the transaction happens synchronously - payment and ownership are exchanged instantly. This is common in shops and the exchange of physical products. It is a well-established historical exchange model, creating a strong emotion around ownership transference and freedom for the consumer.

Continuous observation
The consumer agrees to be observed and monitored continuously in exchange for access to products and services. Numerous companies use this new form of transaction now, but leaders such as Facebook and Google have built up vast advertising capabilities by leveraging this model.

Ch.12

Transaction types and endings.

The beginning of the consumer life-cycle generally starts with a transaction. The type of transaction will characterise the rest of the consumer experience and, especially, the end. It progresses from a simple exchange of currency and value to the establishment of a power relationship that endures throughout the remainder of the engagement. It creates consequences that hide or encourage transparency. It can welcome or deny feedback about the transaction. It can establish partnerships and bonding between provider and consumer. Transaction types are powerful tools for designing experiences and endings.

Five transaction types

There are broadly five types of transaction models used in consumerism. There are, of course, nuances within these five. Sometimes one transaction type is clearly dominant. At other times a transaction might be a hybrid of a couple of different types. However, most consumer engagements can be categorised into one of these five transaction types. These are listed on the left and below in more detail, together with examples.

Payment after delivery

This is a good transaction type for the consumer. They hold the power by not paying for the experience until they are satisfied. In this situation they have leverage. They can feel comfortable giving feedback about the quality and delivery of the transaction. Consequently, it could be considered a transparent and visible type of transaction to use for a consumer experience.

The right types of business can benefit greatly from confident, uninhibited feedback. Capturing it in the right way can yield good results for improving business knowledge and service delivery. In some situations, the consumer can negotiate the price in relation to the quality of the service delivered. These transactions often involve higher customer contact. In a restaurant, for instance, it may well be a single individual who provides the service, such as a waiter. So, there may be an additional reward beyond the payment in the form of the gratuity. This could well empower the consumer to reward enhanced delivery by the provider.

Restaurants

When the payment is being made at the end of the transaction, consumer experiences have the potential to change while being delivered. For example, an important feature of the restaurant industry is the opportunity for selling alcohol to the consumer throughout the meal. Alcohol is a high yield product and produces a good income for the business. Restaurants wouldn't want to limit income by agreeing payment up front. Payment After Delivery provides freedom for changes in the delivery.

PayPal

To ease the emotional anxiety for making purchases, PayPal offers buyers a window to receive and judge their purchases. This lowers the risk for the consumer when buying from unknown suppliers.[1]

Since they are the transaction controller in the exchange between purchasers and many online sellers, PayPal have the opportunity to control standard practices. With the Payment After Delivery service they offer the best for both: the seller receives their money straight away and the buyer won't be charged for 14 days, which provides them with a chance to receive and review the purchase.

Payment before delivery

Paying before the delivery of the experience reduces the consumer's empowerment in the relationship. Transparency is reduced, with the consumer unsure of the details of the service to be provided until its completion. This limits the ability of the consumer to negotiate value or have a frank discussion with the service provider. The customer would usually have to make an effort to have their complaints heard, possibly in some formal, systematic way that further distances the service from the customer.

Fyre Festival

This was described as being an exclusive music festival, scheduled to take place on a remote desert island with beautiful people in attendance. The event became a legendary disaster due to the lack of experience of the founders – it was apparently closer to The Lord of the Flies than an exclusive music festival. Stranded flights, insufficient accommodation, people stealing each other's' beds, only one music act performed, no lighting, no running water... were just some of the issues. Five thousand tickets were sold before the event. The prices varied between US$500 to US$1500 for different packages. There was no one available for customers to talk to. They had no leverage. No one was refunded. Not surprisingly, the festival was subsequently the focus of many lawsuits.[2]

Entertainment

The band Radiohead disrupted the model of payment with their album Rainbows by asking customers to pay what they thought was appropriate. It would have been interesting to extend this to their tour tickets so as to have the entertainment industry's transaction model challenged with a more open alternative.[3]

Train travel

A very common everyday delivery failure for commuters is a late train. Some countries require train companies to pay compensation for a late train. But to receive it, the customer is often required to fill in a form. The UK website ReeClaim.co.uk, allows users of London Transport to reclaim automatically for train delays. They have refunded £1,013,203 since the company started. This is paid automatically, straight into the customer's bank account. Reclaiming is automatic for consumers who have signed up. The company says *"In many cases, trains are delayed without you even realising that you were delayed. In fact, most of our users who received refunds were surprised to learn that they were delayed."*[4]

Scheduled payment

Scheduled payments can be transactions of multiple convenience. They reduce the burden on the consumer for remembering to pay a regular bill, and the business for generating invoices and chasing payment.

Consumers might well have little interest in the transaction, since their impression of the service is reduced to a basic level, thus giving minimum attention to the payment. Thus, low customer engagement is common with this type of transaction. Providers may become complacent, as well as consumers. Scheduled payments do away with many aspects of communication in the relationship. The need to recognise a moment where reflection about the service can take place is reduced – it usually occurs at the end, and therefore cuts back on the opportunity for feedback. This is evident in the press coverage some companies receive while using this transaction type, as exampled in the report below.

Energy industry

A 2016 consumer report by the Competition & Markets Authority on the UK's energy market disclosed some fascinating examples of disengagement with utility companies that use a type of scheduled payment. Out of 7000 domestic retail energy customers the report found that

- 36% of respondents either did not think it was possible or did not know if it was possible to change one or more of the following: tariff; payment method; and supplier.
- 34% of respondents said they had never considered switching supplier.
- 56% of respondents said they had never switched supplier, did not know it was possible or did not know if they had done so.
- 72% said they had never switched tariff with an existing supplier, did not know it was possible, or did not know if they had done so.[5]

Truebill

Scheduled payments can easily be forgotten and remain hidden from the consumer's everyday inspection. It is common for people to only discover they are paying for a subscription when they look through their bank statements in detail. According to Truebill, a financial management service, 84% of people have subscriptions that they have forgotten about.[6] They have got lost in the convenience of the scheduled payment model. Truebill promise to reveal and end forgotten subscriptions. The user synchronises their checking and credit accounts with the Truebill app. The app then looks for subscriptions to find better deals, or unused accounts.

Synchronous payment

This is a transparent form of transaction, because of its immediacy, and respects both provider and customer equally.

Digitising services have increased the use of synchronous transactions. For example, 'pay-as-you-go' services are digitised and are increasing in many sectors. RFID (radio-frequency identification) cards are facilitating more synchronous transactions, for example in transport. Many entertainment services use a synchronous method to provide immediate access to films, music and applications.

The transition to digital, especially with entertainment media, does have its problems. The complicated licences involved in digital media have made ownership a grey area. Digital rights are impacted by location, longevity and type of use. Ownership and transference of assets between people are also a difficult area to resolve.

Many consumers assume they own the iTunes music and films they have downloaded. The transaction model has made them assume this. But legally they have only purchased the right to have access. This right does not behave like the physical product ownership it attempts to mimic. Synchronous payments assume infinite ownership. This is a long way from the truth.

Digital Rights Management (DRM)

In a shock for many Microsoft e-book users, the company announced in April of 2019 that it would be shutting its store - stopping all e-book sales and removing all purchased books from peoples' libraries. The company said users would receive a full refund.

In a recent interview in Wired, John Sullivan, executive director of the non-profit Free Software Foundation, describes the frustration for the consumer with DRM and this type of transaction. *"Once we complete a transaction you can't just reach into my pocket and take it back, even if you do give me money. This is why we call DRM media and devices defective by design or broken from the beginning. There's self-destruction built into the whole concept,"*[7]

A few months later Apple announced at its World Wide Developers' Conference that it would be ending iTunes, moving from a physical product ownership metaphor to one of subscription and licence. This should have been what was presented at the outset in terms of a transaction type. This mix up was reinforced by the types of purchase options established in iTunes with Rent or Buy, which are metaphors from the time of VHS format and Blockbuster rental.

Environmental

The synchronous payment type moves responsibility from the provider to the consumer, since ownership is fully transferred. It maximises freedom to do what the consumer wants with their purchase, especially at the end, which isn't always a good thing. For small, quickly consumed items such as bread, this makes sense. But for larger items that may possibly have a negative environmental impact, this can be limiting, generating chaos at the end. Consumers have the freedom to dispose of their item anyway they want to. The broken link between the provider and consumer also limits governance around environmental matters.

Industries are reconsidering this issue in light of climate change and material responsibility. They are beginning to offer types of purchasing that keep the relationship between them and the consumer tethered. This might include scheduled payments or continuous observation (the 5th payment type). These help to keep aspects of the relationship connected and therefore establish joint responsibility for the asset when the end comes. This helps to reclaim and manage the off-boarding experience in an environmentally sensitive way.

Continuous observation

In a new world that sees data as a currency, people can agree to sell access to what they do, where they go, who their friends are. For the provider, this knowledge informs greater understanding of the customer and improved targeting of adverts. The moment of transaction for the consumer is often overlooked, since it may be embedded deep in terms and conditions. Although the consumer sees many perceived benefits, there is a great deal they relinquish in terms of privacy and transparency when they have little opportunity to engage with the provider directly.

Smart TV awareness

Many consumers are unaware how much they are observed. For example, people overlook the access Smart TVs have into a person's behaviour once they agree terms and conditions. Much of the detail is buried deep behind a little-known term called ACR - Automatic Content Recognition.[8] This observes viewing behaviour and sends it back to manufacturers, who then send it on to third parties. A 2021 article in consumerreports.org, a consumer rights organisation, presented research by Northeastern University and Imperial College London that found *"smart TVs and other internet-connected devices sent data to Amazon, Facebook, and DoubleClick, Google's advertising business. Almost all the TVs sent data to Netflix even if the app wasn't installed or the owner hadn't activated it."[9]*

Delta Air Lines

As technology advances and facial recognition becomes more widespread, businesses investigate expanding observation beyond the online behaviour of customers. An article in the New York Times revealed this predictable expansion of customer surveillance. At Atlanta Airport Delta Airlines piloted a service improvement to reduce waiting times by having face recognition technology check the identities of passengers. This improved service flow by two seconds per person, and nine minutes time loading a plane the company said. 98% of Delta's 25,000 Atlanta customers agreed and signed up. For a business, knowing a person's facial identity and linking that with online behaviour is wonderful for targeting adverts.[10]

How should it feel?

There are a number of approaches to consider when creating an emotionally positive ending for the consumer. The psychology discipline has a wide range of knowledge around endings. Some themes like memory, closure or personal reflection can be aligned to events relating to the end of a consumer experience. For example, behaviours like remembering are important in terms of defining and categorizing an experience in the long term. Gaining closure is important for terminating an experience and moving on from it. And knowing when something is starting to end can help planning and valuing what is good.

In the following pages we look at some psychological themes, their origins and consider their relevance to consumer off-boarding.

Role exit and the crack of doubt

In her book, Becoming an Ex, Helen Rose Ebaugh[1] examines the transition that we experience when moving between roles. In the past we would have had far fewer roles - one marriage, one job, one career, one faith. In modern society we tend to move far more frequently between these roles. Ebaugh, herself an ex-nun, researched a broad range of people who have moved from one role to another – ex-convicts, ex-alcoholics, ex-cops and transsexuals.

She found that in the initial phases of role exit, doubts are often generated by organizational changes, personal burnout, a change in relationships, or the effect of some event. These changes ignite a crack of doubt, which is then reflected to peers as cuing behaviour. If other people then pick up on and recognise the cues, the doubts are reinforced and the crack opens wider, prompting a re-evaluation of the role. Once the individual is convinced that their doubts are valid, they will lay greater stress on the areas under scrutiny. Subsequent events are then considered negatively as a way of reinforcing the crack of doubt. The person will then actively seek new roles - the second stage of role exit.

We can see similar behaviour in consumers as they evaluate their loyalty to a product, service or digital product. If a failure in the product offering or function happens, a crack of doubt emerges. Further negative experiences will then reinforce the crack of doubt and the consumer will seek the end. The crack can be mended. There is plenty of work in marketing and customer experience that looks at service recovery and retention and considers how to stop the crack of doubt.

The consumer off-boarding experience really starts with the crack of doubt. It is hard to predict where it will emerge, and it is difficult to measure since it remains a feeling of the consumer. It is only later that it becomes tangible as a result of actions in the consumer's behaviour. For example, announcing the intention to leave the relationship using a communication channel such as email, or reduced product usage.

Helen Rose Ebaugh's work offers a great deal of insight into the experience of endings. I recommend looking at it more if you feel it might resonate for your product's off-boarding.

Seize and freeze

In a 1996 paper, psychologists Donna M Webster and Arie W Kruglanski,[2] suggested that, humans like to achieve cognitive closure on issues. They seek out definitive answers to ambiguous situations with the aim of increasing accuracy and prediction in a chaotic world.

People tend to want to do this in two ways.

- they seek out closure quickly (the urgency tendency)
- to maintain that for as long as possible (the permanence tendency)

This, the authors believed, helped people 'seize' and 'freeze' when making judgements, which in turn reduces the processing of information.

Seize

Consumers are looking for a timely ending that can be achieved without blockers or diversions that slow their desire to leave or end a consumer relationship. For example, trying to leave a service can be difficult when the route to leaving is purposely ambiguous, contains mis–direction or requires increased effort. Some pay–per–view tv companies demand consumers have a one-hour sales interview before being allowed to leave. This is a massive effort that people tend to avoid. Harry Brignull (we will hear more from Harry later in the book) describes this as a Dark Pattern he calls the Roach Motel – you get into a situation very easily, but then you find it is hard to get out of it. Consumers want to know they can leave easily and smoothly – the urgency tendency.

Freeze

Ambiguity about the ending should be avoided. Consumers are looking for a clearly defined ending that is stable and permanent. Settling accounts and confirming the status of the end is vital to achieving this. For example, back billing which we will hear about later, when energy companies change the cost of a bill after years of it being settled. The consumer wants to trust that settling a bill is permanent - the permanent tendency.

The consumer wants to seize closure quickly and for that closure to be permanent. This can be supported through clear sign posting with transparent and reasonable stages reaching a tangible conclusion. Evidence of the end should be provided as a clear and permanent record of the relationship.

Peak End rule. Designing for the Remembering Self and the end

In his book Thinking Fast and Slow Daniel Kaheman,' talks about the Peak End rule and its relationship to the Experiencing Self and the Remembering Self. [3]

- The Experiencing Self is the one that answers the question *"Does it hurt now?"*

- The Remembering Self is the one that answers the question *"How was it on the whole?"*

The Peak End rule suggests that a person has two moments that they clearly commit to memory. These are the peaks (good or bad) of an experience, created by the Experiencing Self and the end, created by the Remembering Self.

When creating product experiences, businesses and designers tend to focus on delivering a great peak experience. This is not surprising: consumers expect their product experience to be the best it can be. But in the absence of a good ending, the positive memories created with a good peak will be undone by the consumer having a bad experience at the end. Just aiming for peaks is a short-term solution for businesses built on customers that only visit once. It will undermine long term brand equity, as departed consumers won't return, due to the ending they experienced being bad.

Businesses that aim to be around for a long time must imagine their customers leaving and returning over years or even decades. Designing for the Remembering Self and the end can help achieve the long-term strategy of a business. So, when product teams gather and talk about the strategic future or their product, it is good to recap about the gravity of Peak End Rule and the short sightedness of only targeting peaks. In the future the best, most visionary companies will commit time and resources to support the Remembering Self and the end.

Reflective design

In his book *Emotional Design*, Don Norman[4] explains a methodology that helps designers create the most attractive, best functioning and hopefully memorable designs. He calls this emotional design. It is achieved by considering three factors in the design of a product.

- Visceral design > Appearance

- Behavioural design > The pleasure and effectiveness of use

- Reflective design > Self-image, personal satisfaction, memories

Visceral design and behavioural design tend to be overarching principles throughout the consumer journey, but their impact is certainly vital at on-boarding and usage. Reflective design tends to be more impactful at later stages of the consumer experience and syncs with other psychological behaviours that we observe in endings generally. Reflective design seems to be the most complicated, difficult to achieve in mass market consumerism.

Don Norman says that *"Of the three levels, the reflective one is the most vulnerable to variability through culture, experience, education, and individual differences. This level can also override the others. Interpretation, understanding, and reasoning come from the reflective level."*

He continues, *"But the reflective level extends much longer—through reflection you remember the past and contemplate the future. Reflective design, therefore, is about long-term relations, about the feelings of satisfaction produced by owning, displaying, and using a product."*

Reflective design leaves an emotional mark. Visceral and behavioural aspects of it can echo on with a person for longer periods, beyond the boundaries of a tangible, defined product. Reflective design triggers reviews of the past, that may summon wider feelings about a brand and expose a business's long-term potential.

Mood memory

A person's mood can influence how they create memories and how they recall them. Numerous pieces of research have investigated the influence of mood on the human condition and memory. Two particular aspects of this are useful when considering the end of the consumer relationship and how humans recall memories about a consumer experience. Penelope A. Lewis and Hugo D. Critchley explain this neatly in a 2003 paper on the issue. [5]

Mood congruence
"Is a phenomenon in which emotional material is remembered more reliably in moods that match the emotional content of the memories. Remembering all of the negative events of our past lives when depressed is an example of mood congruence."

Mood dependence
"Mood dependence on the other hand, is the facilitation of memory when mood at retrieval is matched to mood at encoding. In mood dependence, remembered material normally has a neutral emotional valence."

When we are feeling happy it is easy to recall pleasant memories. When we are in a negative mood, it is easier to reflect on more negative memories.

In a further observation about mood memory, research by Joseph Paul Forgas[6] in 2007 found that it can affect the quality and concreteness of the persuasive messages produced by a person. Futher still, Myounghoon Jeon found, people in a sad mood produced higher quality, more effective persuasive arguments on issues.[7]

For example, at the end of a product relationship, how the consumer recalls the experience might be influenced by their mood at the time of ending. For product development teams, it raises the importance of creating a good mood at off-boarding so memory recall will be able to attach to positive memories of the wider product experience.

Emotional goodbyes

The small variety of psychological behaviours outlined here can help navigate the complicated emotions that are present for the consumer at off-boarding. Those I have selected provide good starting points for consideration, but you may find others that work for the specifics of your products and customers.

I have created a map to help you see an overview of where these behaviours impact. This can help product teams to target the right mechanisms for improving off-boarding in the consumer lifecycle.

Psychological themes and relation to consumer off-boarding

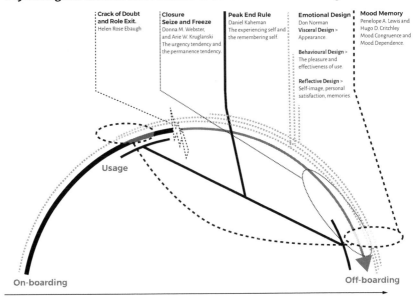

Dark Patterns

A dark pattern is a method of manipulating the intentions of the user by creating an interface that guides them away from things that are against company interests or towards things that are in the interests of the company. For example, you want to leave a service and you can't find the 'close account' link because it is intentionally hard to find.

The descriptor Dark Patterns was coined by the interface designer Harry Brignull in 2010. It was a phrase that has become increasingly relevant as we use more digital interfaces. Harry is now commonly called upon as an expert witness in court cases about Dark Patterns. An increasingly busy job!

In February of 2020 I talked to him about the Dark Patterns theme and how it relates to off-boarding and endings in the consumer experience. First, we discussed the wider categories of dark patterns and how they work. There are around 12 types of Dark Patterns Harry has identified

Types Of Dark Pattern
(courtesy of Harry's website www. darkpatterns.org)

Trick Questions
While filling in a form you respond to a question that tricks you into giving an answer you didn't intend. When glanced upon quickly the question appears to ask one thing, but when read carefully it asks another thing entirely.

Sneak into Basket
You attempt to purchase something, but somewhere in the purchasing journey the site sneaks an additional item into your basket, often through the use of an opt-out radio button or checkbox on a prior page.

Roach Motel

You get into a situation very easily, but then you find it is hard to get out of it (e.g. a premium subscription).

Privacy Zuckering

You are tricked into publicly sharing more information about yourself than you really intended to. Named after Facebook CEO Mark Zuckerberg.

Price Comparison Prevention

The retailer makes it hard for you to compare the price of an item with another item, so you cannot make an informed decision.

Misdirection

The design purposefully focuses your attention on one thing in order to distract your attention from another.

Hidden Costs

You get to the last step of the checkout process, only to discover some unexpected charges have appeared, e.g. delivery charges, tax, etc.

Bait and Switch

You set out to do one thing, but a different, undesirable thing happens instead.

Confirmshaming

The act of guilting the user into opting into something. The option to decline is worded in such a way as to shame the user into compliance.

Disguised Ads

Adverts that are disguised as other kinds of content or navigation, in order to get you to click on them.

Forced Continuity

When your free trial with a service comes to an end and your credit card silently starts getting charged without any warning. In some cases, this is made even worse by making it difficult to cancel the membership.

Friend Spam

The product asks for your email or social media permissions under the pretence it will be used for a desirable outcome (e.g. finding friends), but then spams all your contacts in a message that claims to be from you.

Harry revealed that one of these is used more than any other for avoiding the end - *The Roach Motel*. This is experienced by many people when trying to leave a service. A good example is when you are trying to end an Amazon account.

"You might start from 'Your Account' with the intention to leave. Then overwhelmed by loads of additional information - over 30 direct links. But actually, none would take you to close account. It's a dead end. To delete your Amazon account, you need to go right down to the bottom of the main page, then click 'let us help you'. This will take you to another page and you click 'Need more help'. Then click 'Contact us' - now it gets ridiculous. You are faced with a further 4 options - none say anything about closing the account. You need to click on 'Prime or Something else.' Then an option on 'Tell us more'. Which is a drop-down menu of 13 items. None of which mention closing accounts. You need to click on Login and Security. This reveals a further drop-down menu. And there it is. The first mention of 'Close my Account'. But wait! In order to close the account, you need to have a 'chat' with an Amazon salesperson — who

is there to stop you. Like a big boss at the end of a level game. You can't delete the account yourself. They have to do it for you. You can get in, but you can never leave – like a roach hotel."

Harry outlines examples of good design to avoid dark patterns. He suggests balancing the friction on the way into a product, to the friction on the way out.

clicks in = clicks out

Harry goes on to provide an anecdotal example of industrial resistance to smooth endings.

"While working at a renowned big tech company, I worked on the leaving flow for people closing their accounts. I was suspicious that improvements could be made to the experience, but when proposing ideas, I often came up against the common business paranoia - 'making it easy to leave will increase people leaving'.

Reluctantly I was allowed to propose some improvements and test if they made a difference. Up until this point, a customer leaving this business was asked questions that would push them to further pages, which then presented reasons to stay.

Essentially talking the person out of leaving – a Dark Pattern.

In response, I created an alternative route that would allow the user to leave smoothly and quickly, after which they were asked questions about why they were leaving. The two routes, old and new were tested.

The businesses paranoid fears of customers leaving, never materialised. There was no increase in departing customers. People preferred the quicker route. But the real surprise was the rich data we got on people's reasons for leaving. The new leaving flow became a valuable source of customer knowledge for the business. Proving that people won't leave in larger numbers because a business makes leaving pleasant."

Ch.14

Types of ending.

Ends happen. They will happen to your product, service or digital product. Recognising the characteristics of these endings is helpful for understanding your business, your consumers, their needs and delivering a better-quality product.

When I visit companies and run exercises around the end of a product experience, it is always surprising to me how little conversation there has been about aspects of the product ending. Few people seem to know basics such as - what is the average lifespan of your product? What happens to its material waste? How does the business know when the consumer has stopped using the product?

In this chapter I want to discuss typical endings in the consumer and product lifecycle. I shall be looking at the characteristics of each type of ending. What are the benefits and weaknesses? What examples are available that characterise that particular type of ending? And what are the origins of this behaviour?

There are broadly eight different types of ending that I have listed below in detail. Sometimes a consumer might experience two or even three endings simultaneously, but usually a single one will dominate and define the consumer's experience.

Eight types of consumer ending

	Services	Products	Digital
Time out	2 week holiday, 3 year degree,	Sell by Date. Warranty	1 year software subscription,
Exhaustion /Credit Out	Pay As You Go, Points on your driving license	Battery Empty	Gems in Clash of Clans
Task / Event completion	Parcel delivered, boiler fixed, car serviced, concert watched, operation successful, money transferred	Used disposable items	Game completed
Broken / Withdrawal	Expectation cut short. Break the contract, leave the film early.	Product Broken	Provider has shut down, sold out, gone bust.
Lingering	A pension that you no longer pay into. An unused gym membership.	Old non-fitting clothes. E-Waste old phones in drawers. Changing demographic/age	App deleted yet service capturing data. Unused email accounts. Social media comments and images
Proximity	Move outside of covered area.	Items in loft	Apple to Android. GDPR and LA Times
Cultural	Politics Men only clubs Spotify Alex Jones interview	Kindle Oatly Pepsi Kendall Jenner	MySpace. Yahoo. AOL
Competition	Bigger, Better, Faster	Bigger, Better, Faster	Bigger, Better, Faster

Time Out

A Time Out type ending is a product that is delivered over a fixed period. Such endings could include: a 3-year education course, 2-week holiday, 12-month magazine subscription. Once that period has expired, then so does the service. For physical products, this could be a sell-by-date or a warranty period. For digital products this might be a 1-year subscription to a computer application, or a 24-hour rented film.

Industrial timekeeping

The industrial revolution introduced the modern concept of time, thanks to mechanisation. People moved to the cities in search of work in the new factories. Here time was different: it was divided into three equal 8-hour sections, punctuated by factory clock and bells. These were – work time, your time, sleep time. This increased awareness across societies of defining time, where as previously, in rural communities time had been based on observation of natural cycles of the season, sun and the moon.

Preserving time

Packaging advances meant that food could be preserved for much longer. The tin can was patented by Peter Durand in 1810, who later started the world's first canning factory in England with John Hall in 1846.[1] This extended the life of beef, mutton, carrots, parsnips and soup. It changed the consumer relationship with one of the most common consumer endings - the decay of food.[2]

Agreed time

Holidays require an intensity of scheduling that few people associate with having a relaxing time. There are many time-critical components. You might need to get to the airport 2 hours before departure, the gate before it closes, the car hire office before it closes, and finally, your hotel before bedtime. Then when you get to the end of a holiday, this time-obsessed experience occurs all over again, as we try to move from our holiday location back to home in as quick a time as possible. The whole exercise fails to create an opportunity for reflection at the end. There may well not be a peaceful moment that establishes the fond memories of a good holiday.

Education is another process that has many time-based endings, such as the end of a term, the end of a school year. Many of these events are punctuated with exams. All culminate in graduation and celebration.

Countdown

Decisions over time are one of the most common gaming models. When I was at ustwo, some of the games we created had models that enhanced the decision-making process over a limited period. We also used this same model on trading platforms we created for banking clients. Auctioning is a similar variant of this, when the seller has created a time-based event to intensify the selling experience.[3]

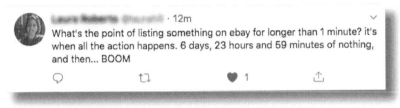

More time, more control

In general, the mobile phone industry emerged out of a traditional telephone industry. With it came the same approach to billing. Consumers were charged for their calls on a per-minute basis. In the UK, it wasn't until Orange was launched in 2005, that increased accuracy of time charging came about. Per-second billing not only changed the perception of time endings for the consumer, it also presented Orange as a company that could measure the details of time.

According to Gerard Goggin, author of Cell Phone Culture, *"Orange innovations like, per second billing, itemised billing free of charge, and direct customer relationships changed peoples' attitudes about telecommunications."*[4]

Clock of the long now

Some people feel that the acceleration of consumerism has broken time into smaller fragments. As a result, we have lost focus on longer periods of time. Certainly, it is proving hard for people to recognise the slow thundering of climate change. Sir David Attenborough has argued that the fixed cycles of governments are too short for long term responsibility on climate change.[5]

This change in our perception of time is the focus of the book The clock of the long now, by Stuart Brand.[6] He argues that humans need to have a clock that recognises and celebrates long views of time. He says *"Such a clock, if sufficiently impressive and well-engineered, would embody deep time for people. It should be charismatic to visit. Interesting to think about. And famous enough to become iconic in the public discourse. Ideally, it would do for thinking about time what the photographs of Earth from space have done for thinking about the environment. Such icons reframe the way people think."* In an ironic twist between the rapid pace of consumerism and the importance of long time, the project is being funded by Jeff Bezos, the founder of Amazon. It is even due to be built on land he owns in Texas.

What we need to consider
- Acknowledge the end date with the consumer early in the process.
- Specify the end date periodically throughout the engagement.
- Remind with increased frequency towards the end.
- Build a crescendo which maximises the experience of the ending.
- Build in moments for reflections.

If executed well, a Time out ending can be a very helpful method for the consumer experience, as it gives clear expectations and opportunities to plan disposal, reflection, and the next sales cycle. If the consumer gets out before the end, this might cause complications, for some, even fines.

Exhaustion / Credit out

Services or products that are based on a numeric value. Once that value is exhausted the service or product end.

Examples included: batteries being discharged, food being consumed, and tyres being run bald. In digital we can see examples of storage being filled up. A currency is common - Dollars, Pounds, Euros, for example. But it may also be represented by a pseudo currency, such as points or credits which have been created by the provider. Some national authorities use a points system such as points on your driving licence (UK) or 3 strikes law in the (US).

Currencies

The exhaustion of currency has characterised peoples' perception of each other for thousands of years. Yet running out of money is common across cultures, race, class and genders. It is probably the most common ending consumers have ever experienced. It is a frequent source of conversations, purpose and exploitation.

In recent centuries pseudo currencies have been seen in loyalty programs. Copper coins were given out to loyal customers by stores to redeem later. Green Shield stamps were very well known in the 20th century. Box-top coupons were often integrated into the product and collected by customers.[7] These locked the consumer into a system where they had to use the chosen pseudo currency of the brand. Once they'd run out, they were like any other consumers again. So, they were downgraded to normal and their loyalty was exhausted.

Physical exhaustion

Ice blocks were an early, tangible and visible system which ended clearly with wet exhaustion. In 1805, Frederic Tudor and his brother came up with a business proposal to ship ice to the West Indies so that people could enjoy a cold drink in the sun.[8] Unsurprisingly, that idea failed. But with a pivot any start-up would be proud of, Frederic decided to sell ice to restaurants and bars instead. With a great deal of effort, he finally established, not only a business but a whole industry of shipping ice. By 1847, 52,000 tons of ice was being moved around the United States.

Industrialisation established brand specificity in consumer products. Where in previous centuries items were unbranded and defined by weight or size, new marketing and packaging changed this. The branded box increased the tangibility of the ending. From *'We are running low on cereal.'* to *'The box of Cornflakes is empty.'*

Some products end when they are full. A full vacuum cleaner bag means that the consumer's vacuum cleaner has a lack of suck when it has reached capacity. Bin bags have similar usage. And as consumerism fills our homes and exhausts our storage, we resort to off-site storage and start again.

Services

Service costs can be expensive and quickly exhaust a person's custom with a company. A clear example can be seen in the US health care system. This becomes difficult for people to afford unless they have insurance cover. According to a recent study, 66.5 percent of all US personal bankruptcies were caused by medical costs. The report estimated that 530,000 families file for bankruptcy every year because of this. Savings are also quickly exhausted without proper cover. A further study by Bankrate, found only 40% of people could even afford a medical expense of $1000 from their savings.[9]

Digitisation

In June of 2000, BT Cellnet launched the world's first General Packet Radio Service, (GPRS).[10] This moved billing from per-minute or second, to billing based on volume of data. This changed the consumers' perception of the pseudo currency. Now they became aware of the exhaustion of data when it ran low. Translating how much data was needed to download a song became a common consumer perception related to the service ending.

Mana

In gaming, Mana has been used as a form of currency for decades. The term goes way back to indigenous people in the South Pacific[11] who used the word to describe a magical force. In gameplay, gaining and losing Mana becomes a source of progression and purpose for the player. So, it is being used for casting magic spells and other game-world activities.

Planning

If there is an inaccurate representation of credit, people get caught out. Fuel gauges are a good example, especially those that estimate the remaining distance. If the consumer drives fast and inefficiently, the remaining distance specified becomes different. This undermines trust in the representation of the currency (fuel). Consumers with electric cars need to plan far more than regular fuel drivers. This is due to the lack of charging stations, the length of charging and the limited range of the charge. Risks like this provide an enormous incentive to plan the exhaustion of your battery.

What we need to consider
- Visibility is key to the credit out / exhaustion type ending.
- Requires a common measure of value or currency.
- A pseudo currency is common.
- Navigating credit can be a source of anxiety.
- Social status can be impacted by low credit/exhaustion.
- Credit out ending is good for a clear sales strategy.
- Conversations gravitate around credit exhaustion.
- Quick repurchase or top-up is key to maintaining loyalty.

Task / Event completion

A previously-defined event offered by the provider (flight to Paris), or a task agreed between the consumer and the provider (fix my tap). Once this event has taken place to the satisfaction of both parties, the service has ended.

This can likewise be applied to products - a disposable coffee cup has a single task and once completed, despite the obvious environmental problems with that, the consumer experiences the end of the product. In digital, games provide an example. A task is presented to the player, they complete that task - maybe a conclusion includes a big-boss fight - and the game finishes.

The ending of the task / event completion varies a great deal. In some cases, it is immediate, forgettable and disposable. In others, it is celebrated, honoured and detailed.

Definition of done

'Task completion has often been misused as a reason for an early celebration. This often happens with politicians. Boris Johnson in the UK saying *'Get Brexit Done'* is an example, or you might remember President Bush announcing an end to combat operations in Iraq while standing in front of a banner saying *'Mission Accomplished'*.[12] This was an image that was often used

USS Abraham Lincoln. Mission Accomplished.
U.S. Navy photo by Photographer's Mate 3rd Class Juan E. Diaz. (RELEASED) wikimedia.org

to criticise his approach in the aftermath of the war.

Another industry that has grappled with the definition of 'done' is the software development industry. Alongside processes like Agile, there are expectations of developers committing code in consistent ways. The question for the product development team is 'How done is it'? Or, as the Agile Alliance website puts it 'I know that you are done, but are you DONE- done?'. This is a similar problem to calling a document on your work server 'Final.doc'. This, of course, gets edited and called 'FINAL_final.doc'. The Agile community has a list of six criteria to meet for code to be defined as done. These are:

- Unit tests passed
- Code reviewed
- Acceptance criteria met
- Functional tests passed
- Non-Functional requirements met
- Product Owner accepts the User Story

Disposability

Probably one of the biggest and most impactful endings is for disposable products. Initially celebrated for convenience in the consumer boom of the 20th century, disposability has now become the scourge of consumerism. The fallout of single-use items with one short function has critically impacted the environment. The ease with which

the experience ends - without friction, instruction, responsibility or reflection - has to change. A great many of these disposable products have fallen outside the waste capturing systems. Their disposal is beyond the care of the consumer or responsibility of the provider. We, as a collective consuming species, have been blinded by this convenient ending. Improvements have been attempted by using biodegradable materials. But these fail to change the underlying behaviour of the consumer or the experience of a badly defined end.

Sadly, more and more products are falling into this category of task event type endings, which are short and disposable. Furthermore, these products are made of increasingly complex materials. Power Hit is just one of many new disposable battery products available for a quick phone charge.

Service industry

A valuable area for the services industry is for the providers to shine at the end of a task done well. Opportunities range from mechanics fixing cars to hotel reception staff saying goodbye. The task event completion is an opportunity to celebrate the completion and embed a good experience with the customer.

Digital

Knowing at a distance that something has been completed has been a useful role in digital systems. The postal service can provide feedback that a letter has been received at a remote destination. Confirmation of a transfer of money reassures a banking customer. Even a tiny graphic indicator can help inform a person that a message has been seen by a recipient. All these provide a sense of closure to the consumer that a task has come to an end.

What we need to consider
- The task or event needs to be defined.
- The end is agreed between parties prior to engagement.
- In products, this may be simple features, even assumptions.
- In services, it might be complex legal negotiations.
- The definition of 'done' needs to be clearly agreed before starting the task or event.
- A task or event ending can be a whimper or thunder.
- Fast disposability may necessitate more friction at the end.

Broken /
Withdrawal

This may be defined as an unplanned, and often uncomfortable separation between the provider and the consumer.

For products, we experience items ending through poor manufacture or exceeding the expectations of normal usage. Common examples could be burning through a pan in the kitchen or finding a newly-purchased item shattered on delivery.

For services, consumers often have to sign some sort of contract. This could be an agreement between the provider and consumer describing the service delivery. Such an agreement usually has a planned type of ending written into it. It might be that a Time Out ending, or a Task/Event has been completed. If the service breaks outside these planned endings, then the situation often gets legal and uncomfortable.

Legislation

An increase in laws in recent years has helped consumers to defend themselves. Privacy laws have empowered digital consumers around the world. GDPR in Europe[13], the California Privacy Act[14] in the US and the updated Act on the Protection of Personal Information (APPI) in Japan[15] have all emerged in the last few years.

There has been an increase in the number of governing bodies and industry watchdogs. These defend customer expectations and set higher industry standards. They may also help the consumer fight bad practice from providers. For example, the UK Energy Ombudsman has recently announced compensation for bad endings, automatically paying customers who have had their switch to a new energy provider go wrong.[16]

Software complexity

In previous generations, complex products might work independently of support for decades. A car or television was a standalone object – beyond the requirement for fuel and electricity. But now many complicated products use software, which is often supported from a remote location. Businesses don't support that software forever, which means that a hidden lifespan is created, which was not mentioned at the on-boarding phase.

Apple has a guideline around the length of supporting products. This should be '5 years after the product is no longer manufactured—or longer where required by law.' They break down these products into two groups thereafter: 'Vintage products are those that have not been manufactured for more than 5 and less than 7 years ago.' 'Obsolete products are those that were discontinued more than 7 years ago.' There are some extreme cases, such as Monster-branded Beats products, which 'are considered obsolete regardless of when they were purchased.'[17] This leaves the consumer of Beats products in a hopelessly vulnerable situation.

Sonos fumbled product endings for thousands of loyal customers in 2019.[18] First with a badly executed e-waste reclaim strategy followed shortly afterwards by an announcement about withdrawing support for legacy products. The issue was publicised on Twitter and Sonos apologised for their poorly thought-through ending.

Services

Wonga was a Pay-day loan company which was launched in 2007. It ended on 30th August 2018, when it went into administration. It was a revered member of the FinTech world, celebrated as a no-nonsense, tech-savvy credit solution. It was the first to provide an instant lending App for Apple mobile phones, with a fully automated, risk processing technology.

Once the dust settled on the business ending, someone needed to sort out the mess. What happened to the customers? Where were the approaches of communication, customer support, legal adherence, etc? These jobs fell to a creditor. A company called Grant Thornton was commissioned to do this work and won the Creditor Engagement Award at the TRI Awards 2019 for it.

Grant Thornton explained that its team undertook a 'multi-pronged approach' to ensure coverage, clarity and consistency, to all customers throughout.[19] There were in excess of two million individuals involved when the collapse happened, so not a small customer base. They created various channels of communication, including email, online updates and SMS campaigns. To do this they drew on a large call centre and clear access to support and answers for worried customers. This aided the resolution of claims and the speed at which they could respond.

Endings after theft

Theft is not an uncommon experience for consumers. Bags may be stolen from bars, bikes from gardens. In the past, insurance has provided a safety net for consumers. Recently, though, technology has provided a different approach. It has enabled the consumer not only to track a stolen device, but to erase content and even kill the device remotely, making it useless for the thief. And, strangely, more empowering for the consumer!

Start-ups shut down

The rapid rise of a start-up concludes more often than not in a shutdown. According to CB insights, 70% of start-up tech companies fail. Most commonly, this occurs around 20 months after first raising finance (with around $1.3M in total funding).[20]

Path has done better than most. It had been going since 2010, but eventually shut its servers down in November 2018, to the disappointment of many of its loyal users.

Making sure the transition for this is as smooth as possible is the honourable thing to do. Some companies pride themselves on how they left. They acknowledge support from their loyal fans and made an effort to transfer data.

Tom Eisenmann, a Professor of Business Administration at Harvard Business School, says that '...shutting down a start-up is almost always a messy affair. One of the worst things a start-up leader can do is exit abruptly, leaving the messy endgame for others to manage'.[21]

What we need to consider
- Broken / withdrawal endings happen as a last resort.
- Expectations have broken, so this ending starts with disappointment.
- Risk assessments can aid preparation.
- It can quickly become a legal matter.
- Stolen items can now be tracked and ended, which makes a far more engaging end.
- Insurance is often sold because of the fear of something breaking.

Lingering

A service or product relationship that has effectively ended due to lack of use yet may still be unknowingly available to the consumer.

Some services become so background to our lives that we forget we are even involved with them. These lingering services may still be capturing data from us while we go about our lives, unaware of their presence. Maybe they still draw a small amount from our bank accounts. Product relationships that were once exciting and used constantly, can change as our needs change. This is evident in clothes that people forget are there at the back of a cupboard. In social media people quickly forget about last month's pictures from a party or a flippant comment they sent in anger. Yet these linger, saved forever, unless actively deleted.

Data

As part of GDPR, consumers have to provide consent for their data to be processed. This means any business with which a consumer has a relationship, has to acknowledge what is happening with the data. But the consumer only needs to provide consent once. Consent does not have an end date, that is, a time when it stops being valid. Companies that you gave permission to just once can still be accessing your data - this could include your calendar, address book, gallery and all sorts of other aspects of your digital life. This gap in an ending can contribute to a lingering relationship.

Micah Hoffman, a principal investigator at Spotlight Infosec, a cybersecurity firm, says *"Understanding what's out there about yourself on the internet, even those things in the past that we've left behind, is very important. When there's a data breach or some other compromise of a system, attackers can grab usernames, passwords, and email addresses, and reuse those credentials to break into other accounts."*[22]

Phones

Many mobile phones are superseded by a new product as the consumer upgrades. The transfer of use from the old to the new often results in the old phone being placed in a drawer, along with numerous other generations of lingering phones. As we heard earlier from the GiffGaff research, the numbers lingering in drawers can be enormous.

Levels of lingering

When the consumer stops using a physical product, they must tolerate its existence until they remove it. It is physically visible in their environment. For example, upgrading a mattress requires removing the old one, otherwise it will clutter up the house or bedroom. Many companies use this issue to improve the sale of a new product. Mattress companies have been removing old mattresses for a while. Ikea have started doing removal as part of their delivery.

Service clutter is less physical. It often only surfaces periodically in bank statements for example. But at least it is there.

Some digital experiences are visible only through functions in settings.

Other lingering assets are entirely invisible to the consumer. For example, carbon impact, un-recyclable plastics, or the processing of unclosed account data could be lingering far beyond user perception or access.

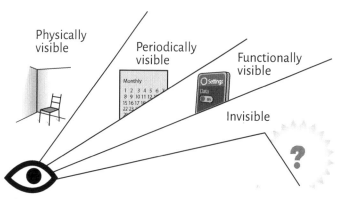

Visibility of lingering assets.

Some companies are starting to provide a service for people to find old accounts and close them down. Unroll.me and justdelete.me[23] helps people find where they have accounts and delete them. But this is far from easy, as the justdelete.me chart shows.

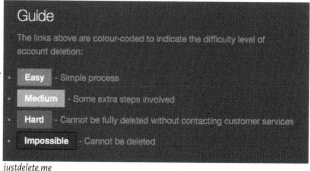

justdelete.me

Batteries

Used batteries may often linger about in the home. They might be tucked away in drawers, out of sight. A good solution is demonstrated in recent product packaging, which encourages the consumer who is getting a new battery to place the old one in the same container upside down. This removes the urge to hide it in a drawer if you haven't got a place for it.

Packaging offers many opportunities for good endings. It is disappointing that so much packaging is designed only as a vehicle for delivery, and not departure.

What we need to consider

· Build in conclusion before the lingering starts.

· Actively conclude and control the end of the product or service.

· Stimulate dialogue when there is reduced usage.

· Remind the consumer that there are options to dispose of the item.

· Clutter is a security risk with unused accounts.

· Lingering, unclosed experiences leave a residue.

Proximity

Moving out of reach of the service or product relationship brings the end.

This kind of ending occurs when the experience ceases because the location has changed. When a person has moved away, they might be outside the distribution of service coverage. In digital, consumers experience a proximity type ending when they move from one digital platform to another. This could be Apple to Android, for example. Apps and data that were once available have now moved out of reach.

For previous generations, consumers would have limited access to fruit and vegetables, based on where they lived. Products from other countries would seem incredibly exotic because they were not available anywhere nearby. Early European access to pineapples, for instance, was only really for royalty.

Avocado

Technology and agriculture techniques have advanced and broken geographical boundaries for many fruit and vegetable products. Nowadays it is common to see fruit and vegetables from across the world at your local supermarket. Consider avocados. They originated in South Central Mexico and even today, Mexico still produces over a third of the world's supply - 34% in 2017.[24] Consumers want them all year round and all around the globe. The UK market, for example, amounted to £51 million in 2012. Keeping up with this demand requires sophisticated storage techniques that extend geographic limits. This is a process in which supermarkets invest enormous effort. An article for The Guardian newspaper, written by Katy Salter, reveals some of the technology utilised. *"Tesco uses a 'bespoke avocado texture analyser', Asda uses 'infra-red to test internal quality', Sainsburys offers Ripe & Ready avocados 'which are 'fully ripened in specialist ripening rooms' and Waitrose try to 'accurately forecasts future demand'"*.[25]

Privacy

An important aspect of proximity is the boundary of privacy. Individuals may feel that their privacy has certain limits. But this is threatened when cookies or other technological methods are found to be digging deeper than the person expected or wanted. This changes their perception of where their privacy ends and their public profile begins. The penny drops when people go to their Google or Facebook Ads page and see how much further their data goes beyond how they had perceived it.[26]

Limited features

In sales promotions, it is common for a trial version of a product to be limited to a certain set of features. The full set is unknown to the consumer until the purchase has taken place. The aim here is to show the capability of the product, but to withhold the full feature set beyond the proximity of the consumer. This tempts them to commit and take the plunge of buying.

Trade traffic

Unbeknown to many consumers, their consumption is dictated to a large degree by trade agreements between countries. This helps to break down proximity boundaries for goods as they travel over borders. This has generated a stark contrast with the UK's departure from the European Union's trade area. To the surprise of many UK consumers, they are now being charged custom fees for goods that they order online, but don't realise they come from Europe.

VPN

A technology that has emerged recently, partially as a result of proximity limitations, is the mass market VPN (Virtual Private Network). Originally, the technology was used by corporations needing increased security for their travelling staff. But more recently, mass- market versions have become popular for people wanting to hide their location, usually to watch TV from other countries. This has invited people to engage in low-level fraud. They pretend they are in one location but seek the benefits of another.

BlackBerry

When Blackberry first came out, it pioneered breaking down the barrier of accessing email on the go with its BBM platform. At its peak in 2013, there were 85 million users. It was so popular and somewhat addictive, that it was often referred to as the Crack-berry. Throughout its growth, it limited its BBM messaging service to Blackberry products only. More recently, messaging apps like Facebook Messenger, WeChat (2019, monthly active users increased to one billion)[27] have achieved success by crossing all platforms. WhatsApp, another cross- platform messenger, was even valued at a lucrative $21.8 billion.[28]

BlackBerry's, proximity-limited product has now ended. The BlackBerry World App store ended in 2019 and OS support for these stopped at the end of 2020.[29]

What we need to consider
- Proximity endings create a sense of exclusion.

- Opportunities are around the transition inside-to-outside the proximity

- Proximity endings are often used in freemium promotions.

- Creating proximity endings can be counterproductive to a good experience.

Cultural

Consumers experience cultural endings of their products, services, or digital products when they perceive them to be out of fashion, or culturally unacceptable.

This could be a service that was previously considered fantastic, but now feels wrong due to social perceptions or a particular look or feel. It could be a product that has a physical style or colour palette that has become less attractive than before. The problem might be a deeper, socially unpalatable point of view about race, gender, or the behaviour of company directors. A whole range of inappropriate points of view can bring an end to product, service, or digital products.

Cultural change is historically slow, steeped in generational differences in attitude. In recent decades such change has moved faster. Many argue that social media has fuelled this acceleration. Some issues are grounded in prejudice and intolerance. Thankfully, these are being challenged more often in society. Others may be based on opinion, taste and aesthetic values: these become interesting areas of nuance.

Fashion
Fashion is a fickle beast. Few areas provide such motivation for purchasing. Yet it can also motivate so many endings. Last season's look can end up squashed at the back of this season's wardrobe. In 1937 the fashion historian James Laver proposed a timeline model of how style comes and goes over the years. Although the fast-fashion of the 21st century would challenge the duration of these dates, the stages are interesting and the language delightful. The model is now referred to as Laver's Law.[30] With a more recent insight into the world of fashion, and its ending Karl Lagerfeld once said: *"Trendy is the last stage before tacky."*[31]

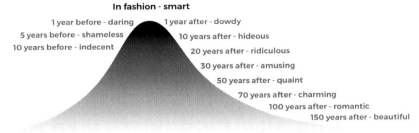

In fashion - smart

1 year before - daring
5 years before - shameless
10 years before - indecent

1 year after - dowdy
10 years after - hideous
20 years after - ridiculous
30 years after - amusing
50 years after - quaint
70 years after - charming
100 years after - romantic
150 years after - beautiful

Laver's Law by James Laver. 1937

Moore's Law

Describing the trend of technical capability, Gordon Moore, co-founder of Fairchild Semiconductor, observed in a 1965 paper, that technical capability in computers doubles every two years.[32] This observation has since set the boundary of what is technically expected by consumers. Falling outside this would be considered a failure. Consumers and the wider marketplace are sensitive to this technical trajectory and its limits.

Uncanny valley

A more human gauge of tolerance is demonstrated in the 'uncanny valley'. First proposed by the robotics professor Masahiro Mori, he suggested: 'As the appearance of a robot is made more human, some observers' emotional response to the robot becomes increasingly positive and empathetic, until it reaches a point beyond which the response quickly becomes strong revulsion.'[33]

Although not a robot, Sonic the hedgehog suffered this fate when the first trailers for the film were released in 2019. These were widely slammed because of his human-like teeth. Many people felt these were not required in the cartoon world. The character, or at least its teeth, had stumbled across the uncanny valley. Faced with ending the film before it had come out, Paramount Pictures listened to the audience, rejigged the release data and removed the uncanny teeth. Sonic was now accepted with his un-human teeth.

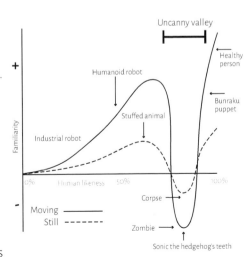

Pepsi ad

Cultural changes can explode if tackled insensitively by businesses and brands. The 2017 Pepsi cola ad with Kendall Jenner[34] flippantly tried to align itself with a protest movement in what seemed, to many to be an astoundingly miscalculated approach. The ad was slammed on social media and in the press. Within a week Pepsi pulled the ad and reconsidered their role in any protest movements.

Cultural attitudes are some of the strongest held beliefs. Clumsy engagement for commercial gain can backfire instantly, specially through social media. And many loyal customer relationships may be destroyed in the process.

Globalisation has meant that some trends are harder to action into new behaviour. Initiatives around smoking took place on national levels. Initiatives around climate change need to be global, not only because the impact is global, but because modern industries operate across global networks. Some of the biggest influences in these customer networks are international brands. So, when poor behaviour by brands is identified, the fall out will be global.

What we need to consider

- Cultural endings are divisive experiences for consumers.
- Consumer research needs to move fast to analyse wider trends.
- Businesses need to be open-minded about changing themselves.
- Businesses need to question if they have a role in sensitive issues.
- A product needs to align socially for current and future audiences.

Competition

The consumer ends one relationship to start a new one elsewhere. They might do this because they see weakness in their current relationship and benefits in another.

The most talked-about aspect of consumer endings is the fear that a customer will go elsewhere. Gargantuan effort goes into discussions about this particular type of ending, generating training and education, articles and books, conferences, boardroom debates. Of all the types of ending that consumers experience, the only one that business cares about is the loss of loyalty to another business. This reveals a deep paranoia of businesses. Some will act appallingly at the off-boarding period in the consumer lifecycle. Behaviour that wouldn't be tolerated in other parts of their business is acceptable. But to avoid a competitive ending, anything goes.

As a result, sales are pressured to hit retention targets instead of improving products. Dark patterns are designed into account closing interfaces, so customers cannot find a way out. Hour-long exercises with sales staff need to be endured before the door is offered to a departing customer.

Industry is so blinded by the important end of the customer lifecycle, that it has left the field of opportunities wide open to the few businesses who approach endings with a strategic vision.

Services legislation

Bad endings have generated legislation. Whether because businesses neglect best practice or something more sinister, Governments have responded by changing laws to make it easier for consumers to leave a provider.

As we heard about earlier in the Benefits for Business chapter with the UK's Current Account Switch Guarantee. It was introduced so consumers could leave their banking relationships more easily. Since its launch in 2013, millions of people have used it to get out of bad banking relationships.

The UK energy industry experienced a similar fate. Its indifference towards good endings was challenged by the Competitions and Markets Authority, who found '56% of customers said they had never switched supplier, did not know it was possible or did not know if they had done so.'[35] Imagine having customers across a whole sector having so little knowledge or feeling they have so little power! Again, endings for consumers were enforced and the Energy Switch Guarantee was created in June 2016.

Digital competition

As part of a wide range of initiatives to increase innovation in the banking sector, Open Banking was created. This saw customer data shared between banks with the use of APIs. The aim was to encourage the Start-up industry to have greater access to the banking market. But this also started the beginning of the end for many customer relationships. Using the APIs meant that consumer could see what another competitor would offer them. This often brought an end to the current relationship.

What we need to consider

· Be cautious of risking long term brand equity against the loss of a customer for one sales cycle.

· Avoid creating dark patterns in closing account processes.

· A consumer leaving your business is a valuable opportunity to gather feedback.

· Don't double down on retention after customers leave. Plough new effort into product development and quality.

7 phases of the end.

The crack of doubt
The first moment a consumer believes that the service or product is not fulfilling their needs.

Acknowledged
Both parties acknowledge the relationship should end.

Actioned
The consumer and provider have an opportunity to action the end.

Observed
Visible or tangible evidence that the end is progressing.

Settled
Confirmation that all is done.

Aftermath
An emotional reflection on what has passed.

Rebirth
Ready for the next cycle.

Phases of the end.

As the consumer relationship comes to an end, a series of events play out. These events guide the consumer as they transition away from the relationship. They can inspire emotional feelings and reactions in the consumer, alongside the delivery of tangible evidence - letters, contracts and messages. Not all phases will happen every time a consumer no longer uses a product, service or digital product. Nor will each phase be equally valued across all consumer sectors. Relationships with products may not emphasize some characteristics as much as those with a service for example.

I have summarised these events into seven broadly definable phases which I have described below, together with examples.

The crack of doubt

The first moment when a consumer believes that the service or product is not fulfilling their needs.

I wrote about role exit and Helen Rose Ebaugh[1] in the first Ends book. It is a key part of the initial experience of ending, I have also explained it in more detail in the chapter called How should it feel? about emotions at the end. The phrase 'crack of doubt' comes from Ebaugh's description of that first feeling that something is ending.

The crack of doubt is hard to define for the consumer until it happens. The run up to the end of a consumer relationship can come about through a collection of nuanced changes in situations. But generally, one issue will push the relationship to the edge.

This is exemplified in personal relationships. It's that moment when one member of a couple does something and it changes the other person's opinion of them. I am sure many of you are familiar with this from early dating experiences. I remember an old girlfriend questioning our relationship because she had seen a certain album on my record shelf. She then questioned my tastes and the match with hers - and subsequently the future of our relationship. It made her change her opinion of me and started a crack of doubt. It turned out I had been given the album as a promotional gift, back when I designed album covers, so was not actually my choice. It could have been the beginning of the end. But it was averted that day. Actually, the end happened a few years later as a consequence of another crack of doubt.

Price comparison sites
One of the most dominating sales innovations of the last two decades has been price comparison sites. These websites were developed for consumers to compare a market of product offerings. Initially, they just compared basic prices offered from comparable suppliers, but, more recently with changes in laws and advancement in technology, the process has become more sophisticated and customer-specific. Now they compare numerous aspects of a product offering.

Many people would assume price comparison sites primarily offer a new consumer relationship. They don't. They end it first. They are efficient customer loyalty killers. They end established relationships by creating a crack of doubt.

As consumers enter the details of a current relationship, the price comparison site will display alternative providers. They present information clearly in a variety of categories, highlighting the offers and improvements from competitors. This starts the crack. The sites then move the consumer through a series of stages with great interface design, digging deeper into offers and finally capturing the consumer in a new deal. This is also where they make their commission! The process is impressively smooth. It offers a coherent and engaging transition from the end of one relationship to the beginning of a new one.

Price comparison sites are one of the biggest sales channels across a wide array of sectors. They can help customers find a new utility company, a phone contract, holiday, car insurance, bank or builder. An article from Warwick Economics Research[2] said the sector achieved £800m ($1.1bn) in 2016 and had grown in the UK by 15% 2015-16. According to the UK's Competition and Markets Authority, 85% of UK consumers have used a price comparison site to end their old consumer relationships.

Knowing more about endings as a business can be very useful. It can open a company's eyes to a wide variety of behavioural reactions in the consumer. It can reveal a degrading relationship or even help understand opportunities in sales. Whole industries now rely on price comparison sites. These are the same industries that have previously overlooked endings.

Acknowledged

Both parties acknowledge the relationship should end.

After the crack of doubt, both parties will seek to formalise the ending. This could be a verbal announcement to service staff for example, asking for the bill in a restaurant. Other arrangements might require the consumer to use a more tangible, traceable method, like a letter. We can see this when people resign from their jobs or give notice as a tenant. This leaves a paper trail, some sort of evidence that a formal procedure is taking place. Such evidence might be part of taking control of old assets or specifying dates for leaving the relationship.

Further on down the process still, digital systems have routes the consumer can navigate themselves as part of a website. Maybe they might log into their account and seek the end by shutting their account via an online interface.

The Acknowledged stage can also be characterised by the type of ending that is already established. For example, if you have car insurance that is paid annually (a Time-Out ending type) the provider might contact you to acknowledge that the end is coming and you should think about renewal. Likewise, if the relationship is a Credit-Out ending, then the provider might contact the customer to inform them that the end has come as they have run out of credit. Either way, an acknowledgement is happening. Parties are informing each other of the end.

Of course, in many physical product relationships, the producer is unaware that the consumer wants to end the relationship. This acknowledgement is for the consumer to formalise emotionally. For example, ignoring all the clothes in your cupboard that don't fit you any more is a lack of acknowledgement. Until the consumer reckons with this emotionally, the end can't be achieved. Action won't be taken. It is one of the reasons the Marie Kondo method is so important in coming to terms with a product ending. In her work as a de-clutter advisor, she encourages her clients to acknowledge the end of an item clearly by saying goodbye to it. This helps to reinforce the end, heighten reflection and take ownership of the ending.

The etiquette of the restaurant bill

The meal is coming to an end. The food has all gone. The wine bottle is empty. There is a natural break in the conversation and you want to acknowledge that with the restaurant staff by getting the bill.

In high end restaurants customers pay for the privilege of setting the pace. That means that at the end they can linger, digesting, chatting. At faster restaurants, with higher turnover of tables, customers do not have that privilege. The bill comes when it is assumed you've finished.

In an article from the Canadian Star newspaper, a couple of experienced waiting staff members reveal the different approaches to getting the bill.

Cheap, fast, assumed, automatic

Leila Ashtari works at a busy, loud and crowded restaurant. There are usually dinners queuing to get in and eat. *"If people want to have another bottle of wine, or if they want to have dessert, I would never ever try to short somebody's evening unnecessarily. But once things are wrapped up, we like to keep the flow, keep things moving,"*

Expensive, sophisticated, attentive, requested

David Taylor is a waiter at a high-end restaurant in Ontario. He has worked in more casual restaurants where he would just bring the bill when the meal was done. But now he would never consider doing that. *"In upscale service, you don't bring the bill until someone has indicated that they want it. Even though it seems intuitive. When people drop a C-note or two (slang term for a $100 banknote in U.S) on dinner, they'd like to purchase the privilege of leisure."*[3]

Announcing the end of the flight

Offering a good service at 30,000 feet requires a great deal of organisation and timing from the flight staff. When the captain announces *"Cabin Crew – prepare the cabin for landing"* it triggers lots of processes for the safety and comfort of the passengers - it is also known as 'Top of the drop' to industry insiders. Flyers will be familiar with the actions required - stow tables, put on seat belts, window blinds up.

An interview with a pilot in Businessinsider.com reveals some of the precisely timed routines.

"Most passengers don't notice the level-off that often occurs when the airplane is about to enter the approach environment or descend below 10,000 feet. When I feel that little level-off for the airplane to slow, I imagine the pilots going through the checklist, and at the right time, I turn to my companion and go 'Ding!' I'm within 4 or 5 seconds well over 50% of the time and it freaks them out."[4]

Break up letter from customers

Aga Szóstek, the author of The Umami Strategy, combined a novel qualitive research method with standard quantitative methods to build rich insights into customer preference. This is a method that could prove useful at off-boarding.[5]

After seeing an article in Interactions magazine – Tech Breakups by E.M. Gerber of Northwestern University, Aga was inspired. It was exactly what she had been looking for to capture emotional sentiment against harder data. But it needed a little adapting for her needs. Where the Northwestern research gave the respondents two letter types – love letter and break up. Although Aga added a third category, – a warning letter, she found the break-up letter inspired customers to share their most honest feelings.

Break-up letter example:
"I can't stand your deceitful advertising. You promise things you're not able to

deliver. You're just a cheat. You take old and long-standing customers for nothing. I've wasted a huge amount of money thanks to you and I will never forgive you. I've never had trust in you, but this time you've overstepped the line. I can't wait to see our contract expire. I'll join the competitors with relish. One thing I regret is spending 20 years with you, wasted."

The method also proved successful with engaging management teams, who usually overlook qualitative research. She now regularly combines feedback from the letters with standard Net Promotor Score information.

Actioned

The consumer and provider have an opportunity to action the end.

After both parties acknowledge that the end is going to happen, events with a purpose start to take place. The participants will be moving beyond words and intentions to changing states and moving matter.

The Actioned phase is probably the most critical point in off-boarding. It can take many forms, but broadly it is the point of no return. Given this importance it might take the form of an endorsement, like signing a legal paper, or clicking a confirm button, or some sort of check.

Taking action is an important experience for the consumer. It can help to embed responsibility, requiring the ownership of consumption's consequences. This might involve the practical exercise of assembling the assets. This could be the simple process of collecting recycling to take to the recycling bins or taking second-hand clothes to the charity shop or packing items to send to an e-bay customer.

Emotionally it can also be a moment of enormous meaning, involving satisfaction and closure. A crescendo to the wider experience, it might also be the most tangible phase in off-boarding. The outcomes might involve more physical assets or clearer actions.

Designing for action at the end

Currently, the approach to recycling is about what material it is made from and the specification that this is recyclable. These are neither emotional nor action-inducing issues. The action of recycling doesn't present the consequences of not recycling. It does not engage with the consumer emotionally. Let's look at two symbols which are generally interpreted as recycling symbols: the Green Dot and the Mobius Loop.

The Green Dot

The Green Dot scheme is run by the PRO Europe (Packaging Recovery Organisation Europe), founded in 1995. It is the umbrella organisation for European packaging and packaging waste recovery and recycling schemes. They describe the purpose of the Green Dot on their website as.

"The Green Dot is the financing symbol for the organisation of recovery, sorting and recycling of sales packaging. When you see the Green Dot on packaging it means that for such packaging, a financial contribution has been paid to a qualified national packaging recovery organisation."[6]

The Mobius Loop

The Mobius Loop was the result of a design competition in the 1970s. It was a good-natured reaction to Earth Day by the Container Corporation of America, a large producer of recycled packaging. They sponsored a competition for art and design students to design a recycling symbol. The winner was Gary Anderson, a 23 year old student at the University of Southern California. The symbol is now universally recognised as the recycling symbol.[7]

Confusion

Too many people think these symbols mean the same thing. This is according to Which?, a consumer magazine in the UK, who conducted research involving 2,155 people. Nearly half the people they asked thought that the Green Dot symbol meant that the item could be recycled.[8] 73% of respondents, knew what the Mobius Loop was, but were unaware it was not universally accepted as recyclable across different countries.

To add to this, Recycle Now, who are the national recycling campaign for England, clarify how unclear it is to the consumer.

"The Green Dot does not necessarily mean that the packaging is recyclable, will be recycled or has been recycled. It is a symbol used on packaging in some European countries and signifies that the producer has made a financial contribution towards

the recovery and recycling of packaging in Europe."[9]

The Mobius Loop creates similar confusion for consumers. *"This indicates that an object is capable of being recycled, not that the object has been recycled or will be accepted in all recycling collection systems. Sometimes this symbol is used with a percentage figure in the middle to explain that the packaging contains x% of recycled material."*[10]

Confusion and lack of purpose are big problems at the end of the consumer lifecycle. We need to provide the consumer with actionable information, not passive information about material capability.

Contact lenses

For so many products, the end can be swift and meaningless. Contact lens are no exception. A recent US study found that 15 to 20 percent of people are flushing their contacts down the sink or the toilet.

Charlie Rolsky, the researcher on the project, said that *"Contact lenses could contribute a load of at least 20,000 kilograms (44,000 pounds) per year."* He claimed that if you add the packaging to the calculation it *"adds about 29 million pounds (13 million kilograms) of polypropylene to the waste from contacts."*[11]

Some lens companies are trying to counter this problem. Terracycle for example, have launched a box that lens users can place in their bathroom. All the material used with contact lens is placed in the box - discarded contact lenses, plastic film, pods, and cardboard packaging. Once filled, the box can be sent back to the producer for sorting and recycling.[12] It is basically an off-boarding box. It continues the consumer / provider relationship and bonds them to recycling and neutralising the consequences of consumption.

Accidental action

In 2016, Marco Marsala posted an enquiry on a user forum called Server Fault.

"I run a small hosting provider with more or less 1535 customers and I use Ansible to automate some operations to be run on all servers. Last night I accidentally ran on all servers, a Bash script with a rm -rf {foo}/{bar} with those variables undefined due to a bug in the code above this line."[13]

As the answers came into his enquiry it was clear he had done something critically devastating to his business. One person described the situation better than others.

"I won't even begin enumerating how many errors are simultaneously required in order to be able to completely erase all your servers and all your backups in a single strike. This is not bad luck: it's astonishingly bad design reinforced by complete carelessness."

Abbreviations and shorthand are quite common in Unix. But they also require experience and knowledge to master and use with confidence.

In Unix language...

- RM = remove
- R = recursive
- F = force removal

The combined "*rm -rf*" means the recursive removal of anything it is pointed at. So, if that is your entire computer, back up and server, then you're in trouble.[14] Not requiring confirmation is risky. So, asking for an actionable confirmation at the end makes a lot of sense and can make all the difference when managing critical situations.

Delete confirmation

In digital products, there are often times when the user needs to delete items. This can happen in a wide variety of contexts, from removal of old files and creating space on burdened hard drives to deleting a digital account. These are important decisions, and most can't be undone. So, it is critical that confirmation is sought from the consumer.

This example from Tumblr is a great example.[15] It is clear about what the consequences are. It is warm and collaborative. And, importantly it requires a confirmation login to approve the deletion.

Observed

Visible or tangible evidence that the end is progressing.

At some point in the off-boarding experience the consumer might be shown a representation of the end happening. This could be the crushing of a plastic bottle, or a graphic depicting the deletion of files, or a piece of paper with evidence that actions are in progress. This is a useful method of informing the consumer of progress and encouraging the idea of closure at the end of the consumer lifecycle.

Sometimes this might be a difficult experience for the consumer to witness. In other situations, it might come as a relief. As an experience it helps to re-enforce a negative situation or a legal status. In other cases, it helps build trust that a conclusion is imminent.

Microsoft UX guidelines

The Microsoft UX guidelines describe how animations can help the consumer observe the deletion of a file. An added level of graphics helps the consumer see the difference between recoverable deleted files and permanently deleted files.

"The progress bar for the Outlook Delete command displays the Recycle Bin for the destination if the files can be recovered, but no Recycle Bin if the files can't be recovered.

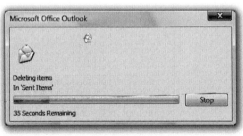

In this example, the lack of a Recycle Bin reinforces that the files are being permanently deleted."[16]

The lack of a destination brings up a recurring problem with deletion of data, which is that there is no evidence to prove the end has happened.

Cutting up credit cards

Some endings might be uncomfortable and shocking to the consumer. Declined credit cards are a good example - these experiences can be embarrassing. In many situations, the consumer has no idea that the end was near for their credit card.

This anecdote from a retail employee at the Hallmark greeting cards store captures the experience from both sides.

"I worked in a Hallmark store back in the mid-1980s. Every month, the banks would publish a book of all the credit card numbers for cards that had been closed prior to expiration for whatever reason — usually non-payment. Before running a credit card transaction for more than a few dollars, we were supposed to check the book. If the customer's card was listed there, then I would make an awkward apology, cut the card in half, and put the two halves under the till in the cash register, where they would sit until they were eventually mailed back to the bank.

I only had occasion to do this three times. Two of the customers were mortified; the third was angry and said he wanted his card back. I meekly explained that technically the card was the bank's, not his, and offered to call the police to settle the matter. He declined the offer.

It's worth noting that the bank paid $50 to any employee who captured a card in this fashion; for a mid-teenage kid in the mid-80s, $50 was quite a prize."[17]

Epson Paper Lab

The Epson Paper Lab[18] is a paper pulper for an office. It takes used paper and processes it to deliver new paper. The whole process takes about 3 minutes. Epson argue that a great deal of energy is lost in the collection, processing and re-distribution of paper, even with well-intended recycling programs. Removing the efforts of picking up wastepaper, processing it at big manufacturing sites and then shipping it to stores is highly impactful.

It also warrants consideration as an experience for the consumer. The difference between throwing away wastepaper in a regular bin or wastepaper in a recycling bin is identical for the consumer, apart from maybe a colour difference of the bin. The processing behind the scenes is invisible. Regular new paper also arrives in the same method as recycled new paper. The Epson Paper Lab reveals the process to the consumer. They can witness the change in the material, from wastepaper being fed into the machine to fresh new paper emerging ready to use. The consumer observes the end of old paper and the rebirth of new.

Re-establishing shot

At the beginning of a film a technique called an establishing shot is often used to show the viewer where they are. According to nofilmschool.com *"An establishing shot is a wide shot that helps the viewer gain knowledge over the time and location of a scene."*

At the end of the film a similar technique is used to recap the story. It often carries a last final poignant message.

Shane (1953). Paramount Pictures

The film Shane (1953), is highly considered for its final scene. After resolving a local feud, the lead is shot and starts to leave town. A young child, Joey, attempts to negotiate with his idol not to leave. After a final farewel,l the lead rides off, while the camera pans out to capture the loneliness of the wide plains of Wyoming, as the child desperately shouts reasons for him to stay.[19]

A crescendo of fireworks

Fireworks have often been a feature of endings. They bring an awe-inspiring visual thrill that helps punctuate an event, bonding large groups of people together in reflective wonder. National holidays and New Year celebrations are common reasons for fireworks. As a world leader in creating experiences, Disney does a great job in bringing an end to a visitor's day.

There are seven daily alternative shows. Some are located around the

Disney Castle, which provides an impressive foreground feature. Others are located around different parts of the parks. They seem to be universally loved by guests, helping to embed memories for years to come. Here is a reaction from a visitor to the Florida park.[20]

wrote a review Jun 2020
📍 Skokie, Illinois • 371 contributions • 21 helpful votes

⬤⬤⬤⬤⬤
Incredible

This firework show is a spectacle that forms a cherished memory, one that you will hold dear for a long, long time. In short: don't miss it.

Read more ▼

However, 2020 park attractions, like everywhere else, have been impacted by Covid, putting the crescendo out of reach for now. As the Disney website puts it - Happily Ever After, Temporarily Unavailable.

Presented by Pandora® Jewelry

Happily Ever After - Temporarily Unavailable

Entertainment located at Magic Kingdom Park

Experience a grand finale to your day with the latest—and most spectacular—fireworks show in Magic Kingdom history.

👪 All Ages

🕐 18 Minutes

⚠ Show Safety, Accessibility and Guest Policies

Settled

Confirmation that all is done

At this point both parties should be feeling satisfied that the end has come. It should resolve the financial debt, the obligations and the material exchange, with the aim of maximising closure. Everyone is being informed that the process is complete, which is vital in keeping the ending clear. It is a great place to summarise experiences, provide financial statements, and is, on many occasions, the last meaningful communication between the provider and the consumer.

At the hairdressers, the person could be leaving the premises and shutting the door. In education, it might be the graduation event where a student receives their diploma. In Facebook, the customer has downloaded their items and waited for 30 days while the account is purged. At the airport, the person has gone through all the security checks and has now emerged out of the doors into the Arrivals hall.

Thanking

It is also a big emotional point and for some, a sigh of relief. For others this is the time to say thanks. Marie Kondo, the declutterer we talked about earlier, says "*When we let go of something we should do so with gratitude*".[21] In her work, she recommends thanking the objects people throw away as a method of valuing them, bringing reflection and creating closure.

According to Harvard Medical school, "*In positive psychology research, gratitude is strongly and consistently associated with greater happiness. Gratitude helps people feel more positive emotions, relish good experiences, improve their health, deal with adversity, and build strong relationships.*"[22] These are all things that businesses would love to be associated with their product experiences, but often do too little work on the 'Thank you' bit.

Settling digital accounts

There is a slight paradox in the process of settling digital accounts when people want them deleted. To inform a person that their data has been deleted would require data about the person to send that confirmation to. It would require account history and contact details. To resolve this, some companies inform the consumer about the procedure with timings, instead of confirming it has happened - *"Your account will be deleted on the 1st of April"*. This solution obviously requires trust in the relationship and lacks the reassurance of a confirmation.

Another issue in data endings is proving something has been deleted. It becomes a burden of proof issue for data businesses to make deletions believable.

Such endings are presenting a tangible end to the data relationship, yet by the nature of the record being deleted, there is no evidence to show to a worried consumer. Providers can present an interface for a request to delete data, then present a process and confirmation of data being deleted. They cannot provide evidence of a deleted item.

Un-settling back billing

Settled accounts should be permanent. Basic levels of trust are shattered when a person is told that what was settled is not the end.

When Shell Energy took over the energy company First Utility, they back-dated customers' bills, in some cases for up to 5 years. People rely on getting closure at the end. It is a critical aspect of trust. Re-opening what is thought to be permanent is shattering to trust.

According to the BBC, in 2019 Clare Crisp received a bill from Shell Energy and saw her bill had sky-rocketed and her direct debit had nearly doubled from £72 to £130. Shell Energy had looked at her bill and believed she had been underpaying since 2014. So, they decided to increase her direct debit without asking.[23]

The UK's Energy Ombudsman banned the practice of back billing beyond 12 months in May 2018. Yet, even in 2019, the first full year of the ban, they still had to resolve more than 2,500 complaints of un-settling back billing.

End of treatment bell

In healthcare, the end of treatment can seem cold and emotionless. The delivery of the news often happens in the same place, by the same person with the same cold method that other less happy news might have generated. There are no balloons or fanfare. For many, this situation can lack closure and emotional conclusion. This is especially difficult for children. So, making the end of that experience meaningful and conclusive is key.

One initiative that can help is the End of Treatment Bell. It was introduced to the UK after a young British girl called Emma had treatment in a US hospital and saw it in action there. While getting her treatment she watched

lots of other kids ring this big brass bell at the end of the ward in celebration of their treatment being completed. When she finished her treatment in the US, she was able to ring it. On returning to the UK, she told the doctors and nurses at her local hospital. They loved the idea and installed one in her ward. When she finished her chemotherapy, she was the first person to ring it.

The Children with Cancer charity, that supports many of the bells installed across the UK, talk about how important it is. *"For a child with cancer, ringing the bell is a huge milestone. It means they've finished their treatment and are ready to get on with life. It's not just a bell — it's a symbol of hope."*[24] The End of Treatment Bell is great at bringing closure. It's noisy, emotional and conclusive. It's a great ending.

Aftermath

An emotional reflection on what has passed

This can be a volatile and difficult period. Emotions aren't always calm and considered or easily captured in data, like other elements of the consumer lifecycle. This time may be reckless and beyond the influence of algorithms. The departing consumer may shriek out their feelings of anger while they are fresh and raw. Other feelings of personal responsibility might be easier to forget.

In the aftermath, consumers are often asked for information about their experience. Generally, this helps inform and improve a company or product. It might aid more consumption by increasing sales with good reviews, or even warning other consumers away with bad reviews. But I won't be adding to the vast information about how to create great reviews here. There are plenty of sources for that information already. I think what might be more valuable in these pages is looking at the wider issue of emotion and meaning at the end of the consumer experience.

Ending episodic grasp of reality

Reuven Feuerstein, an Israeli[25] cognitive psychologist, theorised that without an appropriate organisation of information, people will experience "...*an episodic grasp of reality.*"[26] He describes it further as "...*the world is perceived as consisting of separate, isolated, and unrelated episodes, events, or items. This perception of reality, where there is no organisation, can result in confusion and chaos.*"[27]

The beginning of the consumer lifecycle is orchestrated carefully by the provider to have meaning, detail and emotion. This process assembles separate components together to create a wider consumer experience. The end is different. It is communicated chaotically with many separate, individual experiences, ownership and processes. Meaning is often lost at the end and considered an episode unrelated to the beginning.

Reflection framework

Reflection is a common activity in the period of aftermath. It is a powerful lever for building behavioural change and compliance. Many religions, for example, hold the skill of personal reflection in high esteem. In its strongest form it's an activity of repentance. Historically this helped society to function, pressuring people to reflect on their poor behaviour and to align with a socially acceptable way of life. Repentance, in the Greek etymology of the word, is 'after/behind one's mind'. Or 'to think differently after'.[28]

When we consider the wide field of reflection in psychology, there are aspects that are applicable to endings and the consumer lifecycle. A key rationale for the field of reflective practice, according to the educational psychologist John Loughran, is that "...*experience alone does not necessarily lead to learning; deliberate reflection on experience is essential.*"[29]

We can certainly observe the maximising of experience and a lack of reflection in consumerism. Maybe this also reveals why humans have learnt so little about the impact of consumerism? It is hard to draw links between consumer behaviour and wider impact without reflection being built in.

Structuring a method of reflection for the consumer would require an adaptable and established framework. Borton's Development Framework[30] is used across the world by healthcare professionals – it is prized for its adaptability, helping people to reflect in all types of situations. It is based on three simple questions.

What? So What? Now What?

- What? Prompts the individual to describe what has happened - What did I want? What did I do? What did the provider do? What did the product do?

- So What? Prompts the individual to consider consequences - What was the carbon impact? How does it impact my health? Will my credit rating change? How long will the picture stay online?

- Now What? Prompts the individual to consider actions for the future to improve the situation - I will off-set my flights. I will aim to become fitter. I will reduce my debt. I will manage my social media usage.

Usually, a company will only invite a level of reflection about the 'What?' or 'So what?' questions to prompt a reaction about service or product satisfaction. The ultimate would be a glowing review. But pushing further to the level of 'Now What?' asks for a deeper level of engagement. It invites reflection and responsibility, keeping the wider impact inside the consumer lifecycle. If done together, it bonds the provider and consumer to form a resolution. In turn, it pushes the relationship beyond the short sales cycle of a product to a long-term relationship of joint purpose.

Ikea Buy Back

For decades Ikea has been filling our homes with products. Unless they take action at the end of a product's life and remove it, people won't have room in their homes to buy new Ikea products. So, it's great to see them getting active at the end.

Surprisingly given the quantity of products they sell, Ikea have always taken social responsibility seriously. They aim to be "...a fully circular and climate positive business by 2030."[31] Their latest initiative builds on this previous good work.

The Ikea Buy Back scheme was launched on Black Friday 2020. It invites the consumer to sell back products to the store in exchange for vouchers. This helps the consumer see solutions to their waste issues within the consumer lifecycle, partnered with the provider. This avoids product waste becoming society's problem. As Ikea put it "If it's still in good condition, give it a second life and minimise the contribution to landfill." Ikea have further promised that anything not re-sold will be recycled.

Alumni

Education is increasingly becoming a consumer transaction. Universities now charge students directly and with increased fees. Paying for this privilege also signals the beginning of a borrowing relationship for many students. In the aftermath of graduating there are plenty of changes to adapt to. This can be overwhelming and emotional. Alumnus, plural alumni, is the word used for people who attended a place of study. The Latin origin of the word refers to student. But it is now commonly used for other organisations, businesses[32] or even prisons.[33] For graduates, alumni networks help make the transition between studying and working. They are often involved in, or even facilitate recruitment. This helps a graduate to get that first job and inevitabily-start paying back loans.

One school highly considered for its alumni program is Stanford in California. They have a centre dedicated to their alumni. This includes a business suite, an alumni cafe. It even publishes the Stanford Magazine which provides a common platform for exchange between the school and the alumni beyond.

Businesses, too, are seeing the value in their own alumni network. According to Enterprise Alumni, it is not just about recruitment or a place to moan about old bosses. They say "...*investing in corporate alumni programs increases the sales lead generation and deal closing capability of the organisation.*"[34]

Glassdoor

Glassdoor was launched in 2008 by Robert Barton and Tim Besse. Its aim was to increase workplace transparency by offering employees an opportunity to review their workplace. Initially, this seemed like a great place to vent about your old company. Now Glassdoor has matured and is looked upon as a legitimate resource for job seekers who are looking for a no-nonsense description of a potential workplace.

Glassdoor now has 50 million unique monthly visitors and 70 million reviews of companies, salaries and workplaces.[35] Glassdoor is a perfect place to transition through at the end of a job. It has powerful tools to help a leaving employee to capture their interpretation of their past employer. Like many endings, Glassdoor ushers in beginnings as well. It is now the second biggest job recruitment site in the US.

Rebirth

Emotionally over it, ready for the next cycle, returned to a neutral opinion.

The memory of a consumer experience, much like any other memory, will fade. After the consumer has left the relationship, settled all their accounts and shed their emotions, they will start to feel reborn and neutral again. They will be ready to consider another consumer engagement.

It can take a long time to get to a point of rebirth for a consumer. Zendesk, a customer engagement software company, says *"39% of consumers avoid vendors for over 2 years after having a negative experience".*[36] Of those that will hold grudges, it is the richest customers who hold them the longest *"High-income households are especially prone to hold grudges against businesses that fail to provide a good experience to its customers."*

For the customer, getting over a bad consumer engagement is an emotional experience, a time of complex feelings of injustice and resentment. So, when those emotions fade, it should be considered to be a subtle type of enjoyment for the consumer, who is ready to trust again.

If we are going to deal with the biggest problems in consumerism, responsibility needs to be baked in. The period of Aftermath and Rebirth will become an important place to retain a meaningful relationship between consumer and provider. The relationship after consumption has happened needs to be continued so as to avoid leaving the problems for society to pick up.

In the future, consumers will have to be engaged, for example, with their long-term carbon consequences. Provider and consumer need to be bound together until the impact of that consumption has been mitigated. It could be a lifetime long relationship.

Credit Cards Reborn

How long until you are considered to be new? To be reborn to consume again - at least in the eyes of the provider! According to a recent article in Money Saving Expert, the UK Credit Card industry varies depending on the lender. For example, Nationwide requires a consumer to have been gone 12 months before it will consider them a *"new"* customer. Others have shorter memories. HSBC, for example, will let you have a new credit card after only 6 months. The shortest time any UK lender considers waiting is Capital One, who after only 30 days will give you a new account and card.[37]

How long until you're a 'new customer'?

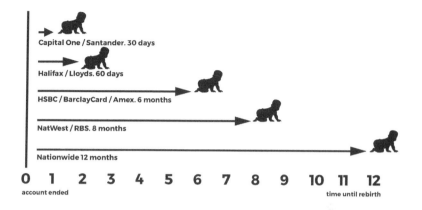

Capital One / Santander. 30 days

Halifax / Lloyds. 60 days

HSBC / BarclayCard / Amex. 6 months

NatWest / RBS. 8 months

Nationwide 12 months

0 1 2 3 4 5 6 7 8 9 10 11 12

account ended   time until rebirth

Carbon legacy for children

Here we come to the most taboo of subjects - the end of you, your kids and your grandchildren and the end of your legacy of consumption. How long does it take? How much carbon gets released as a consequence of you having children?

There is a great deal of discussion about improving our individual consumer habits, but few conversations about reducing our own biological legacy as a method of reduction. Certainly, when I had my kids, it was never considered an issue. Many other things are, but not the carbon impact. Maybe this will change in the future?

A paper by Paul A. Murtaugh and Michael G. Schlax, from Oregon State University, assesses the impact of reproduction and climate change.[38] In their outline they describe its approach. *"Our basic premise is that a person is responsible for the carbon emissions of their descendants. So, for example, a mother and father are each responsible for one half of the emissions of their offspring, and 1/4 of the emissions of their grandchildren."*[39]

Looking at the long-term impact of people's children and grandchildren is a pretty uncomfortable and cold-hearted vision. The privilege we have to bring consumers into the world comes at a climate cost. That cost is eye-wateringly high, according to the paper. If a person in the early 2020's were to adopt good environmental practices - for example like changing their car to electric, travelling less and replacing single glazing with double - they might save about 486 tons of CO_2 emissions over their lifetime. But according to the paper *"...if they were to have two children, this would eventually add nearly 40 times that amount of CO_2 (18,882 t) to the earth's atmosphere."*

Equating some of the data from the Murtaugh and Schlax paper to bad waste products dropped into landfill reveals some worrying consequences for the future.

- Graph A, shows the "persistence of genetic lineages in the United States as a function of number of children produced by the initial parent".

- Graph B, shows the average US lifespan according to the World Bank.

- Graph C, shows how long it takes garbage to decompose according to The Balance.[40]

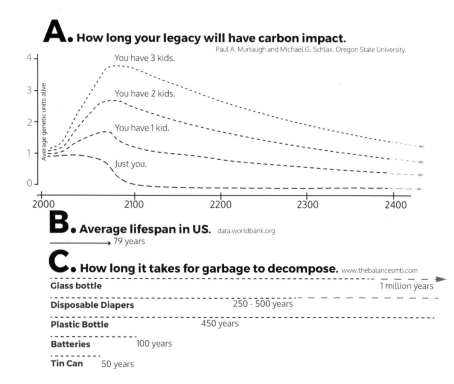

A. How long your legacy will have carbon impact.
Paul A. Murtaugh and Michael G. Schlax. Oregon State University.

You have 3 kids.
You have 2 kids.
You have 1 kid.
Just you.

Average genetic units alive

B. Average lifespan in US. data.worldbank.org
→ 79 years

C. How long it takes for garbage to decompose. www.thebalancesmb.com

Glass bottle	1 million years
Disposable Diapers	250 - 500 years
Plastic Bottle	450 years
Batteries	100 years
Tin Can	50 years

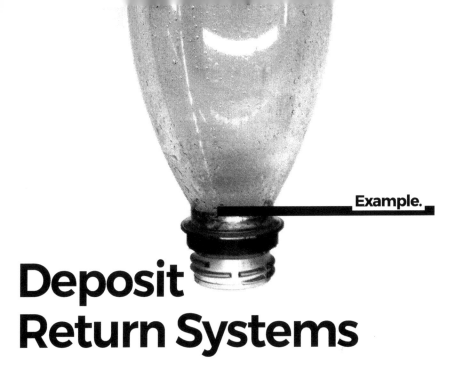

Example.

Deposit Return Systems

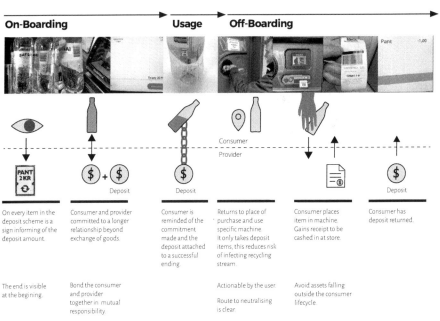

On-Boarding		Usage	Off-Boarding		

Consumer
Provider

Deposit · Deposit · Deposit

On every item in the deposit scheme is a sign informing of the deposit amount.

Consumer and provider committed to a longer relationship beyond exchange of goods.

Consumer is reminded of the commitment made and the deposit attached to a successful ending.

Returns to place of purchase and use specific machine. It only takes deposit items, this reduces risk of infecting recycling stream.

Consumer places item in machine. Gains receipt to be cashed in at store.

Consumer has deposit returned.

The end is visible at the begining.

Bond the consumer and provider together in mutual responsibility.

Actionable by the user.

Route to neutralising is clear.

Avoid assets falling outside the consumer lifecycle.

Bottle deposit schemes are not new. It was common to return glass bottles to the shops in the last century. These early systems were often run with local companies and functioned manually through shop owners and cash returns. The modern versions are national initiatives, run as part of a wider environmental strategy. They are well thought-through industrial decisions involving complex interweaving across recycling sectors, laws around plastics and incentives to industry. But they are also a great example of how powerful a consumer ending can be within a wider initiative. There are over 60 regions around the world who operate a deposit return scheme. [1] They vary, but most retain the same basic features.

The consumer experience

As a consumer experience and especially the off-boarding experience it works well. Right before purchase the consumer is already alerted to the end with the symbol on the packaging. This is reinforced with the deposit being taken on top of the product price. Thereafter the consumer is aware that the empty packaging holds value. This continues to motivate the consumer towards resolving the outstanding debt. They then get the opportunity to go to the recycling machine, often placed at the local supermarket. The consumer puts the empty item in the machine and then receive a receipt that they cash in at the supermarket check-out.

Increased collections

According to Reloop Platform, a circular economy consultancy to governments, *"Collection rates for beverage containers are significantly higher in jurisdictions that have deposit return.*

In Canada, provinces with deposit return programs recover an average of 80% of all non-refillable beverage containers sold, compared to an average of just 50% in provinces that recover containers through municipal curb-side recycling programs." [2]

Consumers want it

Austrians were debating in 2020 whether to establish a deposit return. According to the environmental group, ChangingMarkets.org, the country consumes 34kg of plastic annually, which is more than most other European countries. A recent survey found that 83% of Austrians want deposit return systems.

A further piece of research by the Salzburg government found that 76% of litter along the Salzach in Salzburg city consisted of plastic bottles. [3] This suggests a lack of value for the empty bottle beyond its function to deliver the drink product. This is clearly an alternative ending to the deposit return system experience.

Measuring endings

Another benefit of deposit return systems (DRS) as opposed to other methods is the clear ability to measure. Reloop point out that *"Assessing the performance of a DRS is straightforward since the deposit/refund allows sales and collections to be tracked to the last unit. Measuring the performance of curbside collection programs, on the other hand, is more complex because beverage packaging is collected together with other material, such as paper and non-beverage containers."* [4] Better measuring at off-boarding is key to improving endings.

Ch.16

Start Endineering.

The process below will help you get started creating endings for your products. It references many of the themes and chapters that have been covered in the book and shows how you might start to integrate Endineering into your work.

Current state

How does your product end now?
To dig deeper you will need to look at your current consumer off-boarding experience from a variety of perspectives. This will provide a baseline for improvement.

Define the problems
At the beginning of this book, **The End Gap** chapter outlined four fundamental problems that emerge at the end of the consumer lifecycle. Consider how your business relates to these. Maybe they are all relevant to your product, maybe there are more? Define your situation and expand with details where you can.

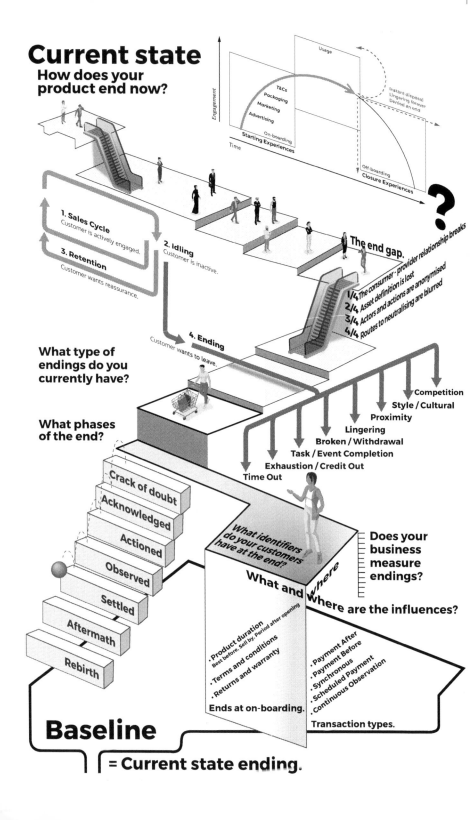

What type of endings do you currently have?

Identify the type of ending that your customers currently experience. The **Types of Ending** chapter provides guidance and explains the characteristics of the eight most common endings. Which ones have most in common with your products?

What is the current route away from your product?

Identify the phases people go through as they leave your product experience. There may be clear functional routes for business efficiency, but what is the experience of these for the consumer? Where are the gaps? How can you improve these moments? More details about this can be found in the **Phases of Ending** chapter.

What and where are the influences?

The consumer off-boarding experience is influenced by events elsewhere in the consumer lifecycle. These frame expectations and position the consumer when the end is reached. Understanding which of those are present in your business is important. Two chapters investigate this in detail – **Ends at On-boarding** and **Transaction Types and Endings**. There are additional mentions about influences throughout the book.

How much do you know about your customer's identity at the end?

Businesses will have varying knowledge about their customers. Some might only know them as a demographic through market research. Others will know them intimately through their digital behaviour. Do you know enough at the end?

The **Accountability and Identity** chapter reveals the need to elevate identity beyond sales and usage, to gain knowledge about impact, legacy, and long-term accountability. Does your business have enough knowledge?

Measuring improvements

How do you currently measure consumer experiences? Are the tools you use appropriate to beginnings and usage periods only? What tools are right for measuring the end in the future? The chapter on **Measuring the End** and sections on **Bias Tools Limit Thinking** are helpful for answering this question.

Assemble the answers from the questions above into a baseline of the current product off-boarding.

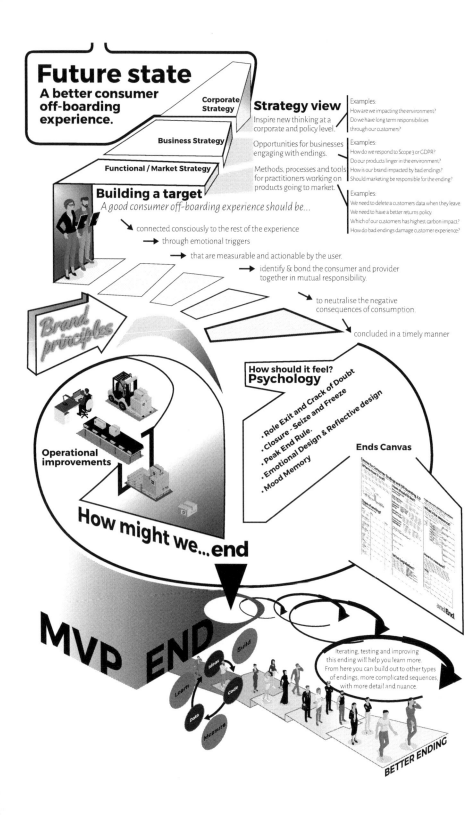

Future state
A better consumer off-boarding experience.

Corporate Strategy

Business Strategy

Functional / Market Strategy

Strategy view

Inspire new thinking at a corporate and policy level.

Opportunities for businesses engaging with endings.

Methods, processes and tools for practitioners working on products going to market.

Examples:
How are we impacting the environment?
Do we have long term responsibilities through our customers?

Examples:
How do we respond to Scope 3 or GDPR?
Do our products linger in the environment?
How is our brand impacted by bad endings?
Should marketing be responsible for the ending?

Examples:
We need to delete a customers data when they leave.
We need to have a better returns policy.
Which of our customers has highest carbon impact?
How do bad endings damage customer experience?

Building a target
A good consumer off-boarding experience should be...

→ connected consciously to the rest of the experience

→ through emotional triggers

→ that are measurable and actionable by the user.

→ identify & bond the consumer and provider together in mutual responsibility.

→ to neutralise the negative consequences of consumption.

→ concluded in a timely manner

Brand principles

How should it feel?
Psychology

• Role Exit and Crack of Doubt
• Closure - Seize and Freeze
• Peak End Rule.
• Emotional Design & Reflective design
• Mood Memory

Operational improvements

Ends Canvas

How might we... end

MVP END

Ideas
Build
Learn
Code
Data
Measure

Iterating, testing and improving this ending will help you learn more. From here you can build out to other types of endings, more complicated sequences, with more detail and nuance.

BETTER ENDING

Future state

How do you plan to create the best possible ending?

Strategy view

Some of the big picture themes in the book are echoing changes happening across the world. The impact of consumerism is a significant issue that many industries and governments are grappling with, and certainly, responsible businesses should be acting upon. This book attempts to inspire new thinking at a corporate and policy level around these themes.

At a macro business level, chapters like **Benefits for Business** directly describe opportunities and issues for businesses engaging with endings. In addition, the chapter **ROI of Ends** attempts to challenge the perception that good endings mean a loss of income.

Most of the book is dedicated to practitioners working on products going to market. Some of the key factors in making this journey a success are revealed throughout the book with examples.

Building a target

The **Aim at the End** chapter summarises some of the wider ambitions captured elsewhere in the book. It assembles these into a statement of intent. It can be useful for you to look at each of the elements in this statement as a sort of check list. How does your business align with these aims?

Brand principles

A good place to start is from your brand principles. No doubt there are characteristics your brand tries to portray: how would these extend to the off-boarding experience? For example, many businesses have 'transparency' or 'authentic' as part of their brand principles. Yet they fail to honour those at off-boarding. How do your brand principles hold up across your product experience, including the end?

Psychology basics

The **How Should It Feel** chapter provides some basic starting points of psychology that can influence the consumer's emotional experience at the end. There are many more, but these give a good baseline for discussion in product teams.

Operational improvements

Are there operational improvements that your business has been looking at, that could be applied at off-boarding? For example, reclaiming materials or legislation – Scope 3 expects businesses to know their product end of life. Knowing all about your company's operational strategy could be a good starting point for improving your product off-boarding.

Innovation

Many of the tools and processes your business currently use for innovation can also be used for creating better endings. For example, using the Design Thinking tool – 'How might we...' is good for synthesising lots of inputs and findings in the creative process. Maybe your business likes to use the Hypothesis Statement tool – 'If this... Then that...' to define any ideas into testable questions. Then maybe building a simple prototype as a Minimum Viable Product is a good first step to start testing, measuring and improving your products endings.

Eventually you should have a clear understanding of all types of endings your products go through. This will build your confidence in delivering the best consumer off-boarding experience for your customers.

Good luck Endineering.

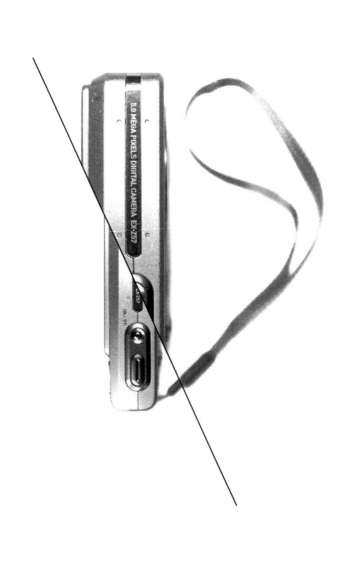

Ch.17
Conclusion.

Now we come to the end of this book, dear reader. I hope that it has changed your thinking. I hope that as a consumer you're inspired to see the potential endings for all the products you buy.

As a professional, I hope you find the strength to ask the simple question about your own products – "*How does it end?*"

My hope is that this book becomes an inspiring resource to answer that question for you and your colleagues. I hope the book becomes a valued and shared resource with your collaborators. I hope it slowly has notes added, pages dog-eared, and generally becomes battered, well used, and even loved.

And then years, maybe decades later, as a result of someone dying and their house cleared it is recycled and pulped into some other useful product.

That would be the best end to this book.

Endnotes.

There are no endnotes for chapters 1, 2, 3, 9, 10 or 16.

Chapter 4. Measuring the end.

1. TTEC. The Value of Individual Customers. Nasdaq TTEC. 2009. https://www.ttec.com/articles/value-individual-customers

2. Brady Porche. The factors of a FICO credit score. CreditCards.com. 2021. https://www.creditcards.com/credit-card-news/help/5-parts-components-fico-credit-score- 6000.php

3. Shoshana Zuboff. The Age of Surveillance Capitalism. Public Affairs. 2019.

4. Wikipedia. Carbon Offset. Wikipedia. August 2021.
https://en.wikipedia.org/wiki/Carbon_offset

5. WebMD. The Dos and Don'ts of Counting Calories. Nourish by WebMD. https://www.webmd.com/diet/features/dos-donts-counting-calories#2

6. Healbe. GoBe3. Healbe. 2019. https://healbe.com/

7. Kyle Wiggers. Healbe claims its GoBe 3 wearable can track calories through the skin with up to 89% accuracy. Venture Beat. 2019. https://venturebeat.com/2019/01/08/healbe-claims-its-gobe-3- wearable-can-track-calories-through-the-skin-with-up-to-89-accuracy/

8. FoodPrint. The Problem of Food Waste. Food Print. 2018. https://foodprint.org/issues/the- problem-of-food-waste/

9. FoodPrint. The Problem of Food Waste. Food Print. 2018. https://foodprint.org/issues/the- problem-of-food-waste/

10. Lily Kuo. 'Operation empty plate': Xi Jinping makes food waste his next target. The Guardian. Aug 2020. https://www.theguardian.com/world/2020/aug/13/operation-empty-plate-xi-jin-ping-makes- food-waste-his-next-target

11. BBC. "China restaurant apologises for weighing customers" BBC News. Aug 2020. https://www.bbc.com/news/world-asia-china-na-53792871

12. EPA National Waste Prevention Programme. Stop Food Waste. Measuring Your Food Waste. 2017. https://stopfoodwaste.ie/planning-shopping/is-that-really-my-food-waste-2

13. Regina Lark. Are there 300,000 things in a Home? A Clear Path. 2017. https://aclearpath.net/are-there-300000-things-in-a-home/ .

14. Neighbor.com. Self Storage Industry Statistics (2020). Neighbor.com 2019.
https://www.neighbor.com/storage-blog/self-storage-industry-statistics/

15. IMDB. Storage Wars. IMDB. 2010. https://www.imdb.com/title/tt1785123/

16. Wikipedia. Municipal Solid Waste. Wikipedia.org. Aug 2021. https://en.wikipedia.org/wiki/Municipal_solid_waste

17. Andrew Sebastian. 5 Countries That Produce the Most Waste. Investopedia. July 2021. https://www.investopedia.com/articles/markets-economy/090716/5-countries-produce-most-waste.asp

18. Wikipedia. Social Credit System. Wikipedia. Aug 2021. https://en.wikipedia.org/wiki/Social_Credit_System

19. Wikipedia. Social Credit System. Wikipedia.org. Aug 2020. https://en.wikipedia.org/wiki/Social_Credit_System

20. China Daily. The era of compulsory garbage sorting begins. China Daily.com. Jul 2019. https://www.chinadaily.com.cn/a/201906/24/WS5d-10650ba3103dbf14329e23.html

Chapter 5. Accountability and identity.

1. Wikipedia. Consumer Identity. Wikipedia.org. Aug 2021. https://en.wikipedia.org/wiki/Consumer_identity

2. Wikipedia. HTTP Cookie. Wikipedia.org. Aug 2021. https://en.wikipedia.org/wiki/HTTP_cookie

3. Jacob Hoffman Andrews. Verizon Injecting Perma-Cookies to Track Mobile Customers, Bypassing Privacy Controls. Electronic Frontier Foundation. Nov 2014. https://www.eff.org/deeplinks/2014/11/verizon-x-uidh

4. Shoshana Zuboff. The Age of Surveillance Capitalism. Public Affairs. 2019.

5. Jacob Hoffman Andrews. Verizon Injecting Perma-Cookies to Track Mobile Customers, Bypassing Privacy Controls. Electronic Frontier Foundation. Nov 2014. https://www.eff.org/deeplinks/2014/11/verizon-x-uidh

6. Jacob Kastrenakes. FCC fines Verizon $1.35 million over 'supercookie' tracking. The Verge. Mar 2016. https://www.theverge.com/2016/3/7/11173010/verizon-supercookie-fine-1-3-million-fcc

7. Sarah Manavis. Why debates about banning online anonymity miss the point. The New Statesman. Feb 2021. https://www.newstatesman.com/science-tech/social-media/2021/02/why-debates-about-banning-online-anonymity-miss-point

8. Eric Barton. What's immoral in business has become harder to define. BBC Worklife. Mar 2015. https://www.bbc.com/worklife/article/20150309-the-danger-of-online-anonymity

9. Eric Barton. What's immoral in business has become harder to define. BBC Worklife. Mar 2015. https://www.bbc.com/worklife/article/20150309-the-danger-of-online-anonymity

10. The World Bank. Inclusive and Trusted Digital ID Can Unlock Opportunities for the World's Most Vulnerable. The World Bank. Aug 2019. https://www.worldbank.org/en/news/immersive-story/2019/08/14/inclusive-and-trusted-digital-id-can-unlock-opportunities-for-the-worlds-most-vulnerable

11. ID2020 Alliance. The Need for Good Digital ID is Universal. Id2020.org. 2020. https://id2020.org/digital-identity#approach

12. Statista. Number of daily active Facebook users worldwide as of 2nd quarter 2021. Statista.com. 2021. https://www.statista.com/statistics/346167/facebook-global-dau/

13. Alfred Ng. How China uses facial recognition to control human behavior. Cnet.com. 2020. https://www.cnet.com/news/in-china-facial-recognition-public-shaming-and-control-go-hand-in-hand/

14. Wikipedia. Anti-mask law. Wikipedia.org. Aug 2020. https://en.wikipedia.org/wiki/Anti-mask_laws

15. Newsweek Staff. The Art of Memorials. Newsweek.com. 2003. https://www.newsweek.com/art-memorials-136063

Tool: Legacy number

1. State of California. Just the facts. Calrecycle. ca.org. 2020. https://www.calrecycle.ca.gov/bevcontainer/consumers/facts

2. State of California. Just the facts. Calrecycle. ca.org. 2020. https://www.calrecycle.ca.gov/bevcontainer/consumers/facts

3. Duncan Clark. How long do greenhouse gases stay in the air? The Guardian. 2012. https://www.theguardian.com/environment/2012/jan/16/greenhouse-gases-remain-air

4. Joe Macleod. When should cookie consent end? AndEnd.co. 2020. http://www.andend.co/blog/2020/11/27/when-should-cookie-consent-end

---

Chapter 6. Benefits for business.

1. Mellissa Chu. The 3 Stages Of Truth In Life. Huffpost.com. 2017. https://www.huffpost.com/entry/the-3-stages-of-truth-in-_b_11244204

2. PT Direct. Attendance, Adherence, Drop out and Retention. PT Direct.com 2016. http://www.ptdirect.com/training-design/exercise-behaviour-and-adherence/attendance-adherence-drop-out-and-retention-patterns-of-gym-members

3. Todd Van Luling. 5 Cable-Cutting Problems You Probably Didn't Think About. Huffpost.com 2019. https://www.huffingtonpost.com/entry/cable-cord-cutting-problems_us_5a81adb9e4b-044b3821fa129

4. Todd Van Luling. 5 Cable-Cutting Problems You Probably Didn't Think About. Huffpost.com 2019. https://www.huffingtonpost.com/entry/

cable-cord-cutting- problems_us_5a81adb9e4b-044b3821fa129

5. Todd Spangler. Cord-Cutting Keeps Churning: U.S. Pay-TV Cancelers to Hit 33 Million in 2018 (Study). Variety.com 2018. https://variety.com/2018/digital/news/cord-cutting-2018-estimates-33-million- us-study-1202881488/

6. Netflix Investors. Netflix's View: streaming entertainment is replacing linear TV. Netflix.net. 2021. https://www.netflixinvestor.com/ir-overview/long-term-view/default.aspx

7. Louis Columbus. 10 Charts That Will Change Your Perspective Of NetFlix's Massive Success In The Cloud. Forbes.com. Jul 2018. https://www.forbes.com/sites/louiscolumbus/2018/07/12/10-charts-that-will-change-your- perspective-of-netflixs-massive-success-in-the-cloud/#66eda61d2303

8. UN University. The Global E-waste Monitor 2020. Ewastemonitor.info. 2020. http://ewaste-monitor.info 9. Metro Tech Reporter. Brits have 55,000,000 unused mobile phones lying around, research finds. Metro.co.uk. 2020.https://metro.co.uk/2020/11/26/brits-have-55000000-un-used-mobile-phones-lying- around-research-says-13657334/

10. Wikipedia. Electronics right to repair. Wikipedia.org. Aug 2021.
https://en.wikipedia.org/wiki/Electronics_right_to_repair

11. Katie Treggiden. Back for good: the fine art of repairing broken things. The Guardian. Aug 2021. https://www.theguardian.com/artanddesign/2021/aug/22/back-for-good-the-fine-art-of-repairing-broken-things

12. Helen Knapman. 7-day bank switching era begins: Full Q&A on what it means for you. Moneysavingexpert.com. 2013. https://www.moneysavingexpert.com/news/2013/09/you-can-now-switch-bank-in- seven-days-time-to-ditch-and-switch/

13. Pay.UK. Current Account Switch Guarantee. Currentaccountswithc.co.uk. 2021.
https://www.currentaccountswitch.co.uk/Pages/Home.aspx

14. EU. Data Protection. Ec.Europe.eu. 2021. https://ec.europa.eu/info/law/law-topic/data-protection_en

15. Wikipedia. California Consumer Privacy Act. Wikipedia.com. 2021. https://en.wikipedia.org/wiki/California_Consumer_Privacy_Act

16. Secretary of California State. AB-375 Privacy: personal information: businesses. California Legislative Information. 2018. https://leginfo.legislature.ca.gov/faces/billTextClient.xhtml?bill_id=201720180AB375

17. Wikipedia. California Consumer Privacy Act. Wikipedia.com. 2021. https://en.wikipedia.org/wiki/California_Consumer_Privacy_Act

18. DataGrail. Mid-Year CCPA Trends Report 2020. Datagrail.io. 2020. https://www.datagrail.io/CCPA_DSAR_H12020/

19. Oliver Milman. What is the polar vortex – and how is it linked to climate change? The guardian.com. 2019. https://www.theguardian.com/us-news/2019/jan/30/polar-vortex- 2019-usa-what-is-it-temperatures-cold-weather-climate-change-explained

20. Wikipedia. Carbon Emissions Reporting. Wikipedia.org. 2021. https://en.wikipedia.org/wiki/Carbon_emissions_reporting

21. GHG Insight. What are Scope 3 emissions? Ghginsights.com. 2020. https://www.ghginsight.com/what-are-scope-3-emissions/

22. GHG Insight. Corporate Value Chain Accounting Reporting Standard. Ghginsights.com. 2020. http://ghgprotocol.org/sites/default/files/standards/Corporate-Value-Chain- Accounting-Reporing-Standard_041613_2.pdf

23. UN University. The Global E-waste Monitor 2020. Ewastemonitor.info. 2020. http://ewaste-monitor.info

24. Joe Macleod. Ends. 2017. Page 202.

25. Byron Sharp, How Brands Grow. Oxford University Press. 2011.

26. Wikipedia. Peak End Rule. Wikipedia.com. 2021. https://en.wikipedia.org/wiki/Peak%E2%80%93end_rule

27. Tamara Scott. Top 10 Predictive Analytics Tools, By Category. technologyAdvice.com. 2021. https://technologyadvice.com/blog/information-technology/top-predictive- analytics-tools/

28. Optimove. Customer Churn Prediction and Prevention. Optimove.com. 2019. https://www.optimove.com/resources/learning-center/customer-churn-prediction-and-prevention

29. Optimove. Customer Churn Prediction and Prevention. Optimove.com. 2019. https://www.optimove.com/resources/learning-center/customer-churn-prediction-and-prevention

30. Interaction Design Foundation. Google's HEART Framework for Measuring UX. Interaction-design.org. 2018. https://www.interaction-design.org/literature/article/google-s-heart-framework-for-measuring-ux

31. Wikipedia. History of smoking. Wikipedia.org. 2021. https://en.wikipedia.org/wiki/History_of_smoking

32. Wikipedia. Tobacco packaging warning messages. Wikipedia.org. 2021. https://en.wikipedia.org/wiki/Tobacco_packaging_warning_messages#United_Kingdom

33. Anthony Rodgers, Alistair Woodward, Boyd Swinburn, William H Dietz. Prevalence trends tell us what did not precipitate the US obesity

epidemic. Thelancet.com. 2018. https://www.
thelancet.com/journals/lanpub/article/PIIS2468-
2667(18)30021-5/fulltext
34. Sarantis Michalopoulos. 'Traffic light' food
labels gain momentum across Europe. Euractiv.
com. 2017. https://www.euractiv.com/section/agri-
culture-food/news/traffic-light-food-labels-gain-
momentum-across- europe/

35. Wikipedia. Pepsi. Wikipedia.org. 2021. https://
en.wikipedia.org/wiki/PepsiCo#Product_nutrition
36. Wikipedia. Carbon Offsetting and Reduction
Scheme for International Aviation. Wikipedia.org.
2021. https://en.wikipedia.org/wiki/Carbon_Offset-
ting_and_Reduction_Scheme_for_International_A
viation

Chapter 7. ROI of Ends.

1. Blake Morgan. 50 Stats That Prove The Value
Of Customer Experience. Forbes.com. 2019.
https://www.forbes.com/sites/blakemor-
gan/2019/09/24/50-stats-that-prove-the-value-of-
customer-experience/#1f7ced524ef2
2. NielsenIQ. Global consumers seek companies
that care about environmental issues. Nielseniq.

com. 2018. https://www.nielsen.com/ca/en/in-
sights/article/2018/global-consumers-seek-compa-
nies-that-care- about-environmental-issues/
3. KPMG. How much is customer experience worth?
KPMG. 2016. https://assets.kpmg/content/dam/
kpmg/xx/pdf/2016/11/How-much-is-custerom-ex-
perience-worth.pdf

Chapter 8. Benevolent beginnings -are they enough?

1. Raoul Adamchak. Organic Farming. Britannica.
2021. https://www.britannica.com/topic/organ-
ic-farming
2. Wikipedia. Silent Spring. Wikipedia.org. 2021.
https://en.wikipedia.org/wiki/Silent_Spring
3. Raoul Adamchak. Organic Farming. Britannica.
2021. https://www.britannica.com/topic/organ-
ic-farming
4. Wikipedia. History of Fair Trade. Wikipedia.org.
https://en.wikipedia.org/wiki/History_of_fair_trade
5. Wikipedia. History of Fair Trade. Wikipedia.org.
https://en.wikipedia.org/wiki/History_of_fair_trade
6. Wikipedia. Food Miles. Wikipedia.org. 2021.
https://en.wikipedia.org/wiki/Food_miles
7. Mark Wilson. The tech industry is terrible for
the environment. These new carbon labels make it
more transparent. Fastcompany.com. 2020. https://
www.fastcompany.com/90516787/the-tech-indus-
try-is-terrible- for-the-environment-these-new-car-
bon-labels-makes-it-more-transparent
8. Tetra Pak. Tetra Pak in figures. Tetrapak.com.
2021. https://www.tetrapak.com/about/facts-fig-
ures
9. Tetra Pak. Life cycle assessment for carton packages. Tetrapak.com. 2021. https://www.tetrapak.
com/sustainability/environmental-impact/a-val-
ue-chain-approach/life-cycle-assessment

10. Tetra Pak. Life cycle assessment for carton packages. Tetrapak.com. 2021. https://www.tetrapak.
com/sustainability/environmental-impact/a-val-
ue-chain-approach/life-cycle-assessment
11. Emily Folk. What the Future of Renewable
Energy Looks Like. Earth.org. 2021. https://earth.
org/the-growth- of-renewable-energy-what-does-
the-future-hold/
12. Wikipedia. Active Disassembly. Wikipedia.org.
2021. https://en.wikipedia.org/wiki/Active_Disas-
sembly
13. Cradle to Cradle Products Innovation Institute.
Green Grows Up: Building in the Age of the Circular
Economy. C2ccertified.org. 2017. https://www.
c2ccertified.org/news/article/green-grows-up-
building-in-the-age-of-the- circular-economy
14. Cradle to Cradle Products Innovation Institute.
Green Grows Up: Building in the Age of the Circular
Economy. C2ccertified.org. 2017. https://www.
c2ccertified.org/news/article/green-grows-up-
building-in-the-age-of-the- circular-economy
15. Charissa Rujanavech, Joe Lessard, Sarah
Chandler, Sean Shannon, Jeffrey Dahmus, Rob
Guzzo. Liam – An Innovation Story. Apple.com.
2016. https://www.apple.com/environment/pdf/
Liam_white_paper_Sept2016.pdf
16. Apple. Apple expands global recycling programs. Apple.com. 2019. https://www.apple.com/

newsroom/2019/04/apple-expands-global-recy-cling-programs/

17. Akanksha Manish, Paromita Chakraborty. E-Waste Management in India: Challenges and Opportunities. Teriin.org. 2019. https://www.teriin.org/article/e-waste-management-india-challeng-es-and- opportunities

18. Silicon valley toxics coalition. SVTC's Mission For A Sustainable Future. Svtc.org. 2018. http://svtc.org/about- us/svtcs-mission-for-a-sustainable-future/

19. Electronics take back coalition. About us. Elec-tronictakeback.com. 2020. http://www.electronicstakeback.com/about-us/

20. Fairphone. We care for people and planet. Fairphone.com. 2021. https://www.fairphone.com/en/story/?ref=header

21. Fairphone. The World's most sustainable smart-phones. Shop.fairphone.com. 2021. https://shop.fairphone.com/se_en/?___store=se_en

22. EeBGuide Project. Transport of wastes to landfill, incineration and recycling facilities – screening and simplified LCA. Eebguide.eu. https://www.eebguide.eu/eebblog/?p=1636

23. Vivienne Walt. Plastic that travels 8,000 miles: the global crisis in recycling. Fortune. 2020. https://fortune.com/longform/plastics-global-recy-cling-problem/

24. Gates Foundation. Bill Gates Launches Rein-vented Toilet Expo Showcasing New Pathogen-Kill-ing Sanitation Products That Don't Require Sewers or Water Lines. Gatesfoundation.org. 2020. https://www.gatesfoundation.org/Media-Center/Press-Re-leases/2018/11/Bill-Gates-Launches-Reinvent-ed- Toilet-Expo-Showcasing-New-Pathogen-Kill-ing-Sanitation-Products

25. Bill & Mellinda Gates foundation. Water, sanitation & hygiene: reinvent the toilet challenge. Gatesfoundation.org. 2013. https://docs.gatesfoun-dation.org/Documents/Fact_Sheet_Reinvent_the_ Toilet_Challenge.pdf

26. Netflix. Inside Bill's Brain. Series 1. Episode 1. 15 mins 28 seconds. https://www.netflix.com/gb/title/80184771

27. Alands Index Solutions. The world's leading climate impact index. Alandindexsolutions.com. 2021. https://alandindexsolutions.com/

28. Doconomy. Climate action in your pocket. Doconomy.com. 2021. https://doconomy.com/en

29. Alison Kirkman. Certified sustainable palm oil is a con. Greenpeace.org.uk. 2019. https://www.greenpeace.org.uk/news/certified-sustainable-palm-oil-is-a-con-says-greenpeace-as-new-evi-dence- links-certifying-body-to-five-years-of-fires-across-indonesia/

Example. Electrolux: Recycled vacuum cleaner

1. Åsa Scherling. Circular Initiative: Collaborations and robotics make the recycling industry a pioneer. July, 2021. https://www.combitech.se/nyheter-in-spiration/press/pressreleaser/circular- initiative-sa-marbeten-och-robotteknik-gor-atervinningsindus-trin-till-foregangare/

2. Electrolux. Designing for new life: The 90% recy-clable prototype vac is here. www.electroluxgroup.com. July 2021. https://www.electroluxgroup.com/en/designing-for-new- life-the-90-recyclable-pro-totype-vac-is-here-33114/

Chapter 11. Ends at on-boarding

1. Krystal Higgins. Bookending with good be-ginnings and ends in the user experience. UXLx: UX Lisbon. 2020. https://medium.com/@uxlx/bookending-with-good-beginnings-and-ends-in-the-user- experience-78bf4bcde963

2. Wikipedia. Food and drug administration. Wikipedia.org. 2021. https://en.wikipedia.org/wiki/Food_and_Drug_Administration

3. Food Standards Agency. Best before and use-by dates. Food.gov.uk. 2021. https://www.food.gov.uk/safety-hygiene/best-be-fore-and-use-by-dates#don-t-trust-the-sniff- test

4. Cosmetics Europe. Understanding the Label. Cos-meticseurope.eu. 2021. https://cosmeticseurope.eu/cosmetic-products/understanding-label/

5. Right to Repair. The French repair index: chal-lenges and opportunities. Repair.eu. 2021. https://repair.eu/news/the-french-repair-index-challeng-es-and-opportunities/

6. GDPR.EU. Cookies, the GDPR, and the ePrivacy Directive. Gdpr.eu. 2021. https://gdpr.eu/cookies/

7. GDPR.EU. Cookies, the GDPR, and the ePrivacy Directive. Gdpr.eu. 2021. https://gdpr.eu/cookies/

8. Digital Trends. Reviews. Digitaltrends.com. 2020. https://www.digitaltrends.com

9. Wikipedia. Sack of Rome. Wikipediea.org. 2021.

Chapter 11. Ends at on-boarding.

https://en.wikipedia.org/wiki/Sack_of_Rome_(410)
10. Wikipedia. Bronze Age. Wikipedia.org. 2021.
https://en.wikipedia.org/wiki/Bronze_Age
11. Jessica Guynn. What you need to know before clicking 'I agree' on that terms of service agreement or privacy policy. Usatoday.com. 2020. https://eu-.usatoday.com/story/tech/2020/01/28/not- reading-the-small-print-is-privacy-policy-fail/4565274002/
12. Wikipedia. Arbitration clause. Wikipedia. org. 2021. https://en.wikipedia.org/wiki/Arbitration_clause
13. Scott Medintz. Forced Arbitration: A Clause for Concern. ConsumerReports.org. 2020. https://www.consumerreports.org/mandatory-binding-arbitration/forced-arbitration-clause- for-concern/
14. Wikipedia. Arbitration Clause. Wikipedia. org. 2021. https://en.wikipedia.org/wiki/Arbitration_clause
15. Layla Ilchi. 11 Stores With Notable Return Policies. Wwd.com. 2019. https://wwd.com/fashion- news/fashion-scoops/11-stores-best-return-policies-fashion-beauty-1203370762/
16. Royal Mail.
Royal Mail names 'mail-back Monday' as the busiest day for returning online purchases and Christmas gifts. Royalmailgroup.com. 2016. https://www.royalmailgroup.com/en/press-centre/press-releases/royal-mail/royal-mail-names-mail-back-monday-as-the-busiest-day-for- returning-on-line-purchases-and-christmas-gifts/
17. Layla Ilchi. 11 Stores With Notable Return Policies. Wwd.com. 2019. https://wwd.com/fash-ion- news/fashion-scoops/11-stores-best-return-policies-fashion-beauty-1203370762/
18. Wikipedia. Returning. Wikipedia.org. 2021. https://en.wikipedia.org/wiki/Returning
19. Sabrina Barr. 'Serial Returners': Confessions Of Shoppers Who Return Worn Clothes To Retailers. Independent.co.uk. 2019. https://www.independ-ent.co.uk/life-style/fashion/serial- returners-con-fessions-asos-harrods-blacklist-shoppers-re-turn-clothes-worn-refund- a8752441.html
20. Klarna. Shop smoother. Klarna.com. 2021. https://www.klarna.com/se/
21. Viglia Giampaoloa, Maras Martab, Schumann Janc, Navarro-Martinez Danield. Paying before or paying after? Timing and uncertainty in pay-what-youwant pricing. University of Portsmouth, Department of Marketing and Sales. 2019. https://researchportal.port.ac.uk/portal/files/13177493/VIGLIA_2019_cright_JSR_Paying_be fore_or_pay-ing_after_Timing_and_uncertainty_in_pay_what_you_want_pricing.pdf
22. Viglia Giampaoloa, Maras Martab, Schumann Janc, Navarro-Martinez Danield. Paying before or paying after? Timing and uncertainty in pay-what-youwant pricing. University of Portsmouth, Department of Marketing and Sales. 2019. https://researchportal.port.ac.uk/portal/files/13177493/VIGLIA_2019_cright_JSR_Paying_be fore_or_pay-ing_after_Timing_and_uncertainty_in_pay_what_you_want_pricing.pdf

Example: Rapanui.

1. Rapanui Clothing. Our Story. RapanuiClothing. com. 2020. https://rapanuiclothing.com/our-story/
2. Ibid.

Example: Stuffstr.

1. Stuffstr. Everything has value. Stuffstr. 2020. https://www.stuffstr.com
2. JackStratten.Why is Stuffstr paying customers to buy back the things it sold them? https://www.insider- trends.com/why-is-stuffstr-paying-custom-ers-to-buy-back-the-things-it-sold-them/#ixzz-6RVH8Ufiw
3. Ibid.
4. Ibid.

Chapter 12. Transaction types and endings.

1. PayPal. What is Pay After Delivery? Paypal.com. 2021. https://www.paypal.com/uk/smarthelp/article/what-is-pay- after-delivery-faq918

2. Wikipedia. Fyre Festival. Wikipedia.org. 2021. https://en.wikipedia.org/wiki/Fyre_Festival

3. Wikipedia. In Rainbows. Wikipedia.org. 2021. http://en.wikipedia.org/wiki/In_Rainbows

4. Reclaim. Automated travel refunds. Reeclaim.co.uk. 2021. https://www.reeclaim.co.uk/

5. Competition & Markets Authority. Energy market investigation. Assets.publising.service.gov.uk. 2016. https://assets.publishing.service.gov.uk/media/576c23e4ed915d622c000087/Energy-final-report-summary.pdf

6. Truebill. The money app that works for you. Truebill.com. 2021. https://www.truebill.com/

7. Brian Barrett. Microsoft's Ebook Apocalypse Shows the Dark Side of DRM. Wired.com. 2019. https://www.wired.com/story/microsoft-ebook-apocalypse-drm/

8. Wikipedia. Automatic content recognition. Wikipedia.org. 2021. https://en.wikipedia.org/wiki/Automatic_content_recognition

9. James k. Willcox. How to Turn Off Smart TV Snooping Features. Consumer Reports. 2021. https://www.consumerreports.org/privacy/how-to-turn-off-smart-tv-snooping-features/

10. Shoshana Zuboff. Surveillance capitalism. Nytimes.com. 2020. https://www.nytimes.com/2020/01/24/opinion/sunday/surveillance-capitalism.html

Chapter 13. How should it feel?

1. University of Houston. Helen Rose Ebaugh. UH.edu. 2021. https://www.uh.edu/class/sociology/faculty/helen-rose-ebaugh/

2. Wikipedia. Closure (psychology). Wikipedia.org. 2021. https://en.wikipedia.org/wiki/Closure_(psychology)

3. Wikipedia. Thinking, Fast and Slow. Wikipedia.org. 2021. https://en.wikipedia.org/wiki/Thinking,_Fast_and_Slow

4. Don Norman. Emotional Design. ResearchGate.net. 2004. https://www.researchgate.net/publication/224927652_Emotional_Design_Why_We_Love_or_Hate_Everyday_Things

5. Penelope A. Lewis and Hugo D. Critchley. Mood-dependent memory. Trends in Cognitive Sciences. 2003. https://web.archive.org/web/20110726013151/http://www.fil.ion.ucl.ac.uk/~plewis/other/Mood- dependent%20memory.pdf

6. Wikipedia. Joseph Paul Forgas. Wikipedia.org. 2021. https://en.wikipedia.org/wiki/Joseph_Paul_Forgas

7. Myounghoon Jeon. Emotions and Affect in Human Factors and Human-Computer Interaction. Academic Press. 2017. https://www.elsevier.com/books/emotions-and-affect-in-human-factors-and-human-

Chapter 14. Types of ending.

1. Christopher McFadden. 27+ Industrial Revolution Inventions that Changed the World. InterestingEngineering.com. 2020. https://interestingengineering.com/27-inventions-of-the-industrial-revolution-that-changed-the-world

2. Tom Geoghegan. The story of how the tin can nearly wasn't. BBC News.com. 2013. https://www.bbc.com/news/magazine-21689069

3. Laura Roberts. Twitter Post. 2019. https://twitter.com/laurahill/status/1200050663658528768

4. Gerard Goggin. Cell Phone Culture: Mobile Technology in Everyday Life. Routledge, 2006

5. BBC News. Sir David Attenborough says fixed-term parliaments lead to lack of climate focus. BBC.com. 2020. https://www.bbc.com/news/science-environment-51252222

6. Wikipedia. Clock of the long now. Wikipedia.org. 2021. https://en.wikipedia.org/wiki/Clock_of_the_Long_Now

7. *Alex McEachern. A History of Loyalty Programs, and How They Have Changed. Smile.io. 2020.* https://blog.smile.io/a-history-of-loyalty-programs

Chapter 14. Types of ending.

8. Linda Rodriguez Mcrobbie. The Surprisingly Cool History of Ice. MentalFloss.com. 2016. https://www.mentalfloss.com/article/22407/surprisingly-cool-history-ice

9. Lorie Knoish. This is the real reason most Americans file for bankruptcy. Cnbc.com. 2019. https://www.cnbc.com/2019/02/11/this-is-the-real-reason-most-americans-file-for-bankruptcy.html

10. This is money. BT buys Securicor's Cellnet stake. Thisismoney.co.uk. 1999. https://www.thisismoney.co.uk/money/news/article-1578327/BT-buys-Securicors-Cellnet-stake.html

11. Pete. In gaming culture, what exactly is mana? KnowGamer.com. 2020. https://knowgamer.com/in-gaming-culture- what-exactly-is-mana/

12. Wikipedia. Mission Accomplished Speech. Wikipedia.org. 2021. https://en.wikipedia.org/wiki/Mission_Accomplished_speech

13. Intersoft consulting. GDPR. Gdpr-info.eu. 2021. https://gdpr-info.eu/

14. Wikipedia. California consumer privacy act. Wikipedia.org. 2021. https://en.wikipedia.org/wiki/California_Consumer_Privacy_Act

15. Andrada Coos. Data Protection in Japan: All You Need to Know about APPI. Endpointprotector.com. 2019. https://www.endpointprotector.com/blog/data-protection-in-japan-appi/

16. BBC news. Energy firms forced to pay £30 for switching blunders. BBC.com. 2020. https://www.bbc.com/news/business-51459525

17. Apple. Obtaining service for your Apple product after an expired warranty. Support.apple.com. 2021. https://support.apple.com/en-us/HT201624

18. Chris Welch. Sonos launches trade-up program for its oldest products. Theverge.com. 2019. https://www.theverge.com/2019/10/30/20939850/sonos-trade-up-program-connect-play-products-discount-offer

19. Grant Thornton. Restructuring 2020. Grantthornton.co.uk. 2020. https://www.grantthornton.co.uk/globalassets/1.-member-firms/united- kingdom/pdf/publication/2020/restructuring-2020.pdf

20. Research Briefs. 378 Startup Failure Post-Mortems. CBInsights. 2021. https://www.cbinsights.com/research/startup- failure-post-mortem/

21. Danielle Kost. How to Recover Gracefully After Shutting Down Your Startup. Harvard Business School. 2019. https://hbswk.hbs.edu/item/how-to-recover-gracefully-after-shutting down-your-startup

22. Thomas Germain. Privacy Fix: How to Find Old Online Accounts. Consumer Reports. 2019. https://www.consumerreports.org/digital-security/how-to-find-old-online-accounts/

23. Just Delete Me. A directory of direct links to delete your account from web services. Backgroundchecks.org. 2021. https://backgroundchecks.org/justdeleteme/

24. Wikipedia. Avocardo. Wikipedia.org. 2021. https://en.wikipedia.org/wiki/Avocado

25. Katy Salter. The myth of the ripe and ready range. The Guardian. 2013. https://www.theguardian.com/lifeandstyle/wordofmouth/2013/feb/19/my-quest-perfectly-ripe-avocado

26. Dylan Curran. Are you ready? Here is all the data Facebook and Google have on you. The Guardian. 2018. https://www.theguardian.com/commentisfree/2018/mar/28/all-the-data-facebook-google-has-on-you-privacy

27. Wikipedia. We Chat. Wikipedia.org. 2021. https://en.wikipedia.org/wiki/WeChat

28. Alison Deutsch. WhatsApp: The Best Facebook Purchase Ever? Invetopedia.com. 2021. https://www.investopedia.com/articles/investing/032515/whatsapp-best-facebook-purchase-ever.asp

29. Rachel Koh. Blackberry OS: Is It Still Surviving In 2019 or It's Dead? Cellularnews.com. 2019. https://cellularnews.com/mobile-operating-systems/blackberry-os-is-it-still-surviving-in-2019-or-its-dead/

30. Denise Winterman. The life cycle of a fashion trend. BBC News Magazine. 2009. http://news.bbc.co.uk/2/hi/8262788.stm

31. Harper's Bazaar Staff. The 80 Greatest Fashion Quotes of All Time. Hapersbazaar.com. 2020. https://www.harpersbazaar.com/fashion/designers/a1576/50-famous-fashion-quotes/

32. Wikipedia. Moore's Law. Wikipedia.org. 2021. https://en.wikipedia.org/wiki/Moore%27s_law

33. Wikipedia. Uncanny Valley. Wikipedia.org. 2021. https://en.wikipedia.org/wiki/Uncanny_valley

34. Alexander Smith. Pepsi Pulls Controversial Kendall Jenner Ad After Outcry. NBCnews.com. 2017. https://www.nbcnews.com/news/nbcblk/pepsi-ad-kendall-jenner-echoes-black-lives-matter-sparks-anger-n742811

35. *Richard Hall. Citizens Advice - Written evidence to Domestic Gas and Electricity (Tariff Cap) Bill Committee. citizensadvice.org.uk. 2018.* https://bit.ly/3vYYaUx

1. University of Houston. Helen Rose Ebaugh. UH.edu. 2021. https://www.uh.edu/class/sociology/

Chapter 15. Phases of the end.

faculty/helen- rose-ebaugh/

2. David Ronayne. Price Comparison Websites. Warwick.as.uk. 2020. https://warwick.ac.uk/fac/soc/economics/research/workingpapers/2015/twerp_1056b_ron ayne.pdf

3. Corey Mintz. What's the etiquette for getting your restaurant bill? Thestar.com. 2008. https://www.thestar.com/life/food_wine/2008/10/21/whats_the_etiquette_for_getting_your_restaurant_bill.html

4. Mark Matousek. 6 small details pilots notice when they fly as passengers that you probably miss. Businessinsider.com 2020. https://www.businessinsider.com/what-pilots-notice-when-they-fly-as-passengers-2018-1?r=US&IR=T#the-planes-landing-routine-5

5. Aga Szostek. Why Brands Should Ask Their Customers To Break Up With Them. www.worldxo.org. 2021. https://www.worldxo.org/why-brands-should-ask-their-customers-to-break-up-with-them/

6. Pro Europe. The Green Dot. Pro-e.org. 2018. https://www.pro-e.org/the-green-dot-trademark

7. Wikipedia. Recycling Symbol. Wikipedia.org. 2021. https://en.wikipedia.org/wiki/Recycling_symbol

8. Plasgran. Consumers don't understand the 'dizzying array' of recycling symbols on their products. Plasgranltd.co.uk. 2019. https://plasgranltd.co.uk/consumers-dont-understand-the-dizzying-array-of-recycling- symbols-on-their-products/

9. Recyclenow. Recycling Symbols Explained. Recyclenow.com. 2020. https://www.recyclenow.com/recycling-knowledge/packaging-symbols-explained

10. Recyclenow. Recycling Symbols Explained. Recyclenow.com. 2020. https://www.recyclenow.com/recycling-knowledge/packaging-symbols-explained

11. Feel Good Team. Contact lenses and plastic pollution – How to properly dispose of your lenses. Feelgoodcontacts.com. 2018. https://www.feelgoodcontacts.com/blog/contact-lenses-and-plastic-pollution

12. *Terracycle. Contact Lenses and Packaging. Teracycle.com.* 2020. https://www.terracycle.com/en-GB/zero_waste_boxes/contact-lens-packaging-en-gb

13. Andrew Griffin. Man Accidentally 'Deletes His Entire Company' With One Line Of Bad Code. Independent.co.uk. 2016. https://www.independent.co.uk/life-style/gadgets-and-tech/news/man-accidentally- deletes-his-entire-company-with-one-line-of-bad-code-a6984256.html

14. Giles Quenot. Questions. Stackoverflow.com. 2013. https://stackoverflow.com/questions/14542441/what- does-rf-in-rm-rf-stand-for

15. Jen Maggio. Tumblr's delete account confirmation modal. Reallygoodux.io. 2020. https://www.reallygoodux.io/blog/tumblrs-confirmation-modal

16. Microsoft. Progress Bars. Docs.microsoft.com. 2020. https://docs.microsoft.com/en- us/windows/win32/uxguide/progress-bars

17. Mark Phaedrus. Have you ever had a declined credit card cut up in front of you? Quora.com. 2019. https://www.quora.com/Have-you-ever-had-a-declined-credit-card-cut-up-in-front-of-you

18. Epson. The Sustainable Way To Securely Destroy And Upcycle Paper. Epson.eu. https://www.epson.eu/paperlab

19. Wikipedia. Shane (film). Wikipedia.org. 2021. https://en.wikipedia.org/wiki/Shane_(film)

20. Tripadvisor. Happily Ever After Fireworks. Tripadvisor.com 2020. https://www.tripadvisor.com/Attraction_Review-g34515-d253208-Reviews- Happily_Ever_After_Fireworks-Orlando_Florida.html

21. Marie Kondo. Sparking Joy. Episode 1. Netflix. 2021. https://www.netflix.com/gb/title/81231940

22. Harvard Medical School. Giving thanks can make you happier. Health.harvard.edu. 2021. https://www.health.harvard.edu/healthbeat/giving-thanks-can-make-you-happier

23. Lora Jones. Energy customers hit with backdated bills. BBC.com. 2020. https://www.bbc.com/news/business- 51005983

24. Children with Cancer UK. The first End of Treatment Bell in the UK. ChildrenWithCancer.org.uk 2020. https://www.childrenwithcancer.org.uk/stories/the- end-of-treatment-bell/

25. Wikipedia. Reuven Feuerstein. Wikipedia.org. 2021. https://en.wikipedia.org/wiki/Reuven_Feuerstein

26. Mandia Mentis. Bridging Learning. UK.sagepub.com. 2009. https://uk.sagepub.com/sites/default/files/upm-binaries/28666_Mentis_Ch1.pdf

27. Mandia Mentis. Bridging Learning. UK.sagepub.com. 2009. https://uk.sagepub.com/sites/default/files/upm-binaries/28666_Mentis_Ch1.pdf

28. Wikipedia. Repentance. Wikipedia.org. 2021. https://en.wikipedia.org/wiki/Repentance

Chapter 15. Phases of the end.

29. Wikipedia. Reflective Practice. Wikipedia.org. 2021. https://en.wikipedia.org/wiki/Reflective_practice#cite_note-Loughran-3

30. Borton, T. Tool for reflection. Bda.uk.ac. 2001. https://www.bda.uk.com/uploads/assets/071c9b28-7e02-4559-b14130f4745006df/cpdreflecttool.pdf

31. BBC News. Ikea to buy back used furniture in recycling push. Bbc.com. 2020. https://www.bbc.com/news/business-54531619

32. Wikipedia. Alumnus. Wikipedia.org. 2021. https://en.wikipedia.org/wiki/Alumnus

33. Prisoners Education Trust. Join the alumni network. Prisonerseducation.org.uk. 2021. https://www.prisonerseducation.org.uk/get-support/people-leaving-prison/join-alumni-network/

34. Enterprise Alumni. Corporate Alumni Platform. Enterprise Alumni. 2021. https://enterprisealumni.com/alumni-dictionary/corporate-alumni-platform/

35. Glassdoor. About Us. Glassdoor.com. 2021. https://www.glassdoor.com/about-us/

36. Zendesk Blog. The business impact of customer service on customer lifetime value. Zendesk.com. 2013. https://www.zendesk.com/blog/customer-service-and-lifetime- customer-value/

37. Helen Saxon. Old Credit Cards. Money Saving Expert. 2017. https://web.archive.org/web/20170918005120/http://www.moneysavingexpert.com/credit-cards/cancel-unused-cards

38. *Paul A. Murtaugh, Michael G. Schlax. Reproduction and the carbon legacies of individuals. https://www.biologicaldiversity.org/ 2009. https://www.biologicaldiversity.org/programs/population_and_sustainability/pdfs/OSUCarbonStudy.pdf*

39. Paul A. Murtaugh, Michael G. Schlax. Reproduction and the carbon legacies of individuals. https://www.biologicaldiversity.org/ 2009. https://www.biologicaldiversity.org/programs/population_and_sustainability/pdfs/OSUCarbonStudy.pdf

40. Rick Leblanc. The Decomposition of Waste in Landfills. Thebalancesmb.com. 2021. https://www.thebalancesmb.com/how-long-does-it-take-garbage-to-decompose-2878033

Example: Deposit Return Scheme.

1. Tomra. Deposit return schemes for collecting drink containers for recycling. Tomra.com. 2020. https://www.tomra.com/en/collection/reverse-vending/deposit-return-schemes

2. Reloop. Deposit Return Systems. Reloopplatform.org. 2020. https://www.reloopplatform.org/wp-content/uploads/2020/03/Fact-Sheet-Performance-20March2020.pdf

3. Changing Markets Foundation and Break Free From Plastic Movement. Plastic Pollution Lobby. ChangingMarkets.org. 2020. http://changingmarkets.org/wp-content/uploads/2020/05/CM_PLASTIC-POLLUTION-LOBBY_FinalEN.pdf

4. Reloop. Deposit Return Systems. Reloopplatform.org. 2020. https://www.reloopplatform.org/wp-content/uploads/2020/03/Fact-Sheet-Performance-20March2020.pdf

Index.

Made in United States
Troutdale, OR
06/14/2023